Old Elland: The Old
Lucy Hamerton

Foreword

It's been so long since Olde Eland was
published it has become very difficult and
expensive to obtain a copy. With this book I
want to address this. As I sit at my desk
writing this, the year is 2019. I wonder if
Lucy would recognise the town she so
clearly was passionate about. So much has
changed and is changing, some things
remain the same. Lucy now has a building
named after her "Hamerton Court" and
many of her beloved streets have gone,
cleared in the 60's to make way for utopian
tower blocks which unlike this book, have
not aged well.

The excellent work of Lucy Hamerton is
now public domain in terms of copyright
thanks to its age and it's time for the world
to have the opportunity to read the
wonderful and rich history of Elland as
expressed back in 1901. There's a great deal
of information presented in this book and it
is invaluable for anyone wishing to learn
about Elland and its history.

Much has changed since 1901 and moreso since the 1600's. The English Language is forever evolving and some of things in this book do not read well, but are presented as found, in the same way Lucy presented the writings that she found, as she found them, despite the challenge they present.

It has taken a great deal of time and hard work to bring this book to you and I'm thankful to everyone who has lent a hand, especially my children who let me use time which is usually exclusively for their attention, to complete this project.

With LOVE.

Granville Fisher.

This page is Intentionally left blank

Olde Eland
being
reminiscences of Elland
by Lucy Hamerton,
together with chapters on the
Antiques of Elland
by
J.W. Clay, F.S.A., etc., etc,
Preface
by Ernest Winter, rector of Elland.
Illustrated
W.H. Gledhill, printer, Westgate,
1901

PREFACE.

BUT for the persistent importunity of a few persons who shall be nameless, this book would never have seen the light. Two great difficulties barred the way. In the first place the writer's unaffected humility caused her to shudder at the very idea of seeing her own name "actually printed" on the title-page of a volume bound in leather or even in cloth, and secondly, she naturally felt a strong-disinclination to enter the arena of authorship at a time when she had long since passed her " three-score years and ten."

These difficulties were in no way removed by assurances that the book would certainly be interesting, or that it would be easy to write, or that it would be "sure to pay"; but they vanished at the mere mention of the word "duty." That it was the authoress' duty to write this book there can be no doubt, because no one else could have written it, and because, had it not been Written, much of what it records Would soon have passed out of memory, to the lasting loss of our local folk-lore. Happily, the duty has been discharged, and the verdict as to Whether it has, or has not been adequately discharged, may be safely left in the hands of the reader.

I have been called upon to write a Preface, not because I possess any special fitness for the task, but because of my official position as Rector of the Parish, and in this capacity, while I cannot hope to write anything worthy of the contents of the book, 'I can at any rate avow that I have a three-fold pleasure in being allowed to write at all. 1st.
It's a real pleasure to have the opportunity of acknowledging publicly, and on behalf of successive generations of people,
the devoted services which the writer, her sister (the late Miss Emma Hamerton) and other members of her family have rendered to the Church. For two sisters to have taught and superintended in the same Sunday School for 60 years without a break, is indeed a record which is seldom

reached, and this was only one out of many branches of their active work. Under successive Incumbents, who held divergent views and had varying methods, their labours continued with unwearying patience and unswerving loyalty. Allusion is made in the book to the dissolving or rather to the suspending, by death, of that long and loving partnership, and mention may fitly be made here of the fact that the survivor still continues her good work with undiminished zeal. Elland is grateful to the authoress and to her family not only for What they have done, but for what they have been-examples, to their shepherds as well as to their fellow-members of the Flock of Christ.

2nd.

It is a pleasure to commend this book because its subject-matter mainly centres round the Church of "Olde Eland." There are, of course, but few to whom S. Mary's can be what it has been and still is to the authoress who knows it stone by stone, but an eight years' happy ministry allows ample time for a merely architectural interest in such a building to develop into veneration

VIII

and deepen into love; and any record (like this) which tends to throw light upon its long history and to preserve its old associations cannot fail to be welcome to anyone who is called to be mainly responsible for its safe custody and care.

3rd.

It is a pleasure to assist, even in a small way, in the production of this book because one of its objects, though not its only one, is the raising of funds for the New Church of All Saints', Elland. Funds are still sorely needed for' the great work that has been taken in hand, and it is gratifying to know} that the entire profits from the sale of this book will go to that object. Many generous gifts have already been received, but among them there has been no more welcome contribution than this free-will offering of the memories of seventy years. The authoress has given to the Church in many other ways, and she hopes that her book may be accepted as evidence of her further desire still to do What she can. I confidently anticipate that "Olde Eland" will command a ready sale. I am sure that the book will he prized by all who have the privilege of personal acquaintanceship with its writer; I believe that it will reach the large circle of those who are connected by ties of family or residence, with Elland and Elland Church; and I trust that it will make its way far beyond the range of our old Church bells, and find favour with that still larger constituency of people who love to help forward the work of extending the Church, the Kingdom of God.

I desire to re-echo the thanks which are elsewhere expressed," to J. W. Clay, Esq., for his chapters on the Antiquities of Elland, and also to my senior colleague for placing his facile pen at the authoress' disposal. The book has involved no little labour, but from cover to cover it has been a labour of love; Its main chapters have been written, not in hours that would otherwise have been spent in dignified ease, but in moments snatched from days that many would deem to be already overcrowded with work; its subsidiary chapters have been penned in the midst of the many duties which are inseparable from the chief-magistracy of an important Borough; and its illustrations represent not a little " midnight oil" freely burnt by one, of whose manifold activities this parish is to be all too soon deprived.

Once more I commend this book to the generous acceptance of Elland's many friends,

for the Sake of its writer, its subject-matter, and its object.

E. W.

THE RECTORY, ELLAND,
S. Mark's Day, 1901.

CONTENTS.

XII

XIII

Part II.

¢ LIST OF ILLUSTRATIONS

"

NOTE.

I RECORD with grateful thanks the kind help afforded

me by many persons during the time that this book has been in preparation.

In the first place to Mr. Clay ; whose admirable chapters on the Antiquities of Elland give it a unique value which it could not otherwise have had ; indeed, it is not too much to say that it was owing to his kind help that the book was completed.

In the next place to Mr. Winter for his great kindness in undertaking to write the Preface.

But many others have helped also; notably Miss Fraser in writing out my first notes; Miss Hawley in giving constant personal assistance; Miss L. Tate in providing notes about several points of interest; and I would further thank especially Mr. John William Brook. Mr. Robert Dempster, Mr. Jonathan Dodgson, Mr. G. Hodson and Mr. A. Townsend, who have furnished valuable aid in the way of information or illustration;

This page is Intentionally left blank

1 INTRODUCTION.

Introduction

There is both pleasure and pain in looking back on the old, old days, but Elland having been my home for so many years is endeared to me by these memories of the past as' no other place could ever be ; and as I scarcely think Elland itself would he were it not for the dear old Church, under the shadow of which I was born, and where I have

had the privilege of worshipping for over seventy years.

My father, John Hamerton, of this town, was the son of John Hamerton, of Fold, in Shibden-dale, and afterwards of Staups, Northowram, and the great grandson of John Hamerton, of Peel House, Warley. He was educated first at the Grammar School, Stockport, and afterwards studied at Guy's and St. Thomas's Hospital, Whilst they Were united. He came to Elland in 1815 and lived with his aunt, Mrs. Greenwood, at West House, until 1821, When he married Mary Rushforth, daughter of Joseph Rushforth, of Hill Top, (now known as North House), and went to live at the Cross, next to the Parsonage, and there I was born on March 8th, 1824.

We were first allowed to attend afternoon Service at the age of five, and well I remember our rejoicings when, on Sunday mornings, the Church "loosed," as the expression is, and We saw the congregation coming out.

It is said that the first doctor who came to Elland hoped to establish a very good practice, having no rival, but he soon left in despair, and when questioned as to his reasons for not remaining said, "Elland people never needed a doctor, as the "posnet" was scarcely ever of the fire and they applied an oatmeal poultice inwardly every morning, and another every evening, so doing away with all need of drugs." At the time of my father's coming to Elland, Mr. Hiley was the only medical practitioner in the place, but my father's practice extended to Golcar, Longwood, Lindley, Norland, Stainland,.Greetland, Brighouse, Scammonden, Rishworth, &c.

We left our old home at The Cross in 1830 for West House ; until 1834 we had a governess, and then my sister and

I were sent to school at Southport ; strange little creatures We must have looked when starting on our Journey. I remember we were dressed in nankeen pelisses, and little cottage bonnets, very simply trimmed with brown. We travelled to Southport partly by stage-coach, partly by chaise, and sometimes had to change conveyances as many as eight times,--a method of travelling Which would now be considered very tedious and uncomfortable, especially in the cold of a "real old-fashioned winter," and over so exposed a road as Blackstone Edge ; this was, however, a great advance on my mother's experience, Who went to her first school riding on a pillion, behind her brother; her elder sister riding in the same manner behind her father, and their Iuggage-very little no doubt, according to present-day Ideas-being carried behind a man-

servant. A pillion was a kind of was a kind
of little hard mattress cushion, fastened
behind an ordinary saddle, on which
children or ladies were able to ride, and
when a lady rode behind a man-servant he
had a belt strapped round his waist for her to
hold.by.

Sometimes in returning from Southport we
had to come in a barge on the Duke of
Bridgwater's canal as far as Knott Mill, near
Manchester, and very much we enjoyed the
greater part of our water journey, but as we
neared Knott Mill we were disgusted with
the blackness of the canal ; we used to tell
our mother that we might dip our pens in
and write with it, little thinking that our own
beautiful clear river at Elland would one day
be in the same sad state.

I think my pleasantest recollection

of a journey is of one taken when I was eight years old ; at that time I had a severe illness, but was sufficiently recovered in May to be able to go out, and the beauty of the Spring foliage and blossoms I can never forget. When able to travel I was taken to Redcar, driving all the way, while my little sister was consoled for not being able to go with me, by being taught by our grandmother to make button-holes and to stitch, the work being made easier for her by the use of pink thread. We drove first to Leeds, where We stayed the night, and next morning went on through Harewood, where I well remember the beauty of the trees. Beautiful, also, was the common at Harrogate, and most of the scenery as we passed through Knaresboro', Thirsk, and Northallerton, not far from where we saw the ruins of Mount Grace, and the conical hill of Rosebery Topping. What a great pleasure it would be to take that drive again! At Redcar, I first saw the sea, and when some time after there was a great flood in the Calder, with quite large waves, I told my sister that if she would place her hands on either side of her face so as to hide the land she would know what the sea was like.

While at school we were prepared for Confirmation by Mr. Jackson, the incumbent of Trinity Church, but were not confirmed until we came home, where the preparation was finished by Mr. Atkinson and Mr. Fraser. We were confirmed at Halifax, by Dr. Longley, Bishop of Ripon; the Parish Church was full of candidates, many of whom walked into Halifax from the out-lying districts. I was then sixteen, my dear sister fourteen and a half. We did not return to school, and only studied in a very desultory way at home. At that time we began to teach in the Sunday school, the girls being then taught in Mrs. Grace Ramsden's school, behind the Church. The boys' school Was at one time held in What is now called the "Old Prison," then it was removed to a large room in Casson Place, now a plumber's shop, and afterwards to the old Baptist Chapel in Jepson Lane, Which is now the "Parish Room." Sunday school teaching was then a very different thing from what it is now, for the children of working people had little or no chance of learning even to read and write on week-days, as they had to go to work when very young, and that not for a few hours a day, but from early in the morning until late at night. Our old nurse, Jane Lumb, who

The Old Parsonage

This page is Intentionally left blank

lived with us forty-nine years and three months, has often told us how she used to go to work at Greetland when only five years old; she was too tiny to walk such a long distance, so one of the men who worked at the same place took pity on her, and carried her each way. 50 Sunday school teaching meant usually teaching the scholars to read. I remember teaching mine from a 'Reading made Easy,' with a pictorial alphabet at the end, shewing how 'A was an Archer and shot at a Frog &c.; but this was religiously pasted down by the superintendent as likely to make the children inattentive, the pictures being so much more attractive than letters which, as yet, meant nothing to them.

There was then no "Whitsunday Treat," but at Christmas every scholar had a half-penny book and a bun,---re wards which were often valued more than the handsomest prizes are now, When Whitsuntide was first celebrated by a school feast, the scholars were re-galed in the large room in Casson Place, where the Boys' school was held, While I believe the teachers had a tea" at the Savile Arms, and for long after the school Feast became an institution the scholars had coffee and buns, but the teachers an elaborate tea. '

Some time after we began to teach in the Sunday school Elland was arranged in districts for Tract distributing, when we had New Street, with our mother, as a district, and went in turns with 'an Aunt to Little Bradley, Raw Royds, and Brow Bridge.

In 1841 or 1842, the Sick Club was begun by Miss Caroline Atkinson and

Miss Wiglesworth, the greater part of the necessary fund being raised by subscriptions from honorary members, but the Club has succeeded so well, and is still in such a flourishing condition, that these are not now needed. In the early days there were Quarterly Teas for the members, but they have long been exchanged for an Annual Meeting, where

such business as the election of officers is transacted.

At the close of the Crimean War I was in London; and there had an experience I have never forgotten. I and my cousin were sitting with the windows open, when she said suddenly "Listen ! there are the cannon - that means Peace" The end of a great war was a wonderful thing to us even then, though we knew little or nothing of it in comparison with what is now known of passing events however distant.

We went on our first visit to Oxford very shortly after, and saw the beautiful illuminations in honour of the Peace. The whole range of windows in University College were lighted with rows of ' candles, and there was a Maltese cross in gas over the door. St. John's had gaslights along the string-course, and Queen's College and Balliol displayed the electric light which was then so costly as to be very rarely seen. All the Colleges and University Buildings were illuminated with gas, oil-lamps, or candles, and many private houses also displaying similar signs of rejoicing, the whole was a memorable sight.

I afterwards saw the fireworks in London from Primrose Hill, but did not go through the City for a closer exam-'

ination and I heard that even little Elland had determined to do its best and had illuminated the Church Tower with blue lights, and Westgate was also illuminated by my brother and sister with blue lights burnt in little cups.

Oxford was very gay that June, there were balls and parties innumerable, but in the whole town there was only one' cab, so we had to be wheeled out! to our evening gaieties in bath-. chairs, like those still in use for invalids.

Jenny Lind was then in England for the second time, and was singing in Oxford during our stay there ; we heard her in the third part of the " Creation," and she did indeed sing gloriously. The Prince Consort, Prince William of Prussia, and the Prince Regent of Baden, were also in Oxford, and the

and she did indeed. sing gloriously. The Prince Consort, Prince William of Prussia, and the Prince Regent of Baden, were also in Oxford, and the

two latter had the degree of D.C,L.
conferred upon them.

Another time of great public re. joicing was
the marriage of . the Prince of Wales, in
March, 1863, when the loyalty of Elland
was shewn by decorations, feastings, and
processions. A large square column,
prepared to represent Aberdeen granite was
placed in the centre of the "The Cross," and
from that three elliptic arches broad enough
to walk upon were carried to the
surrounding buildings. Over the centre was
erected a large dome, about eight feet high,
with a finial on the top, and the whole was
decorated with evergreens and flowers,
while hanging from the centre of each
archway was a large basket of evergreens
and flowers. The ninety yards of wreathing
which this decoration required was made in
my

aunt's laundry, and very joyfully we completed it. At night the dome and archways were lit up by over 2,000 gas jets, a beautiful sight, which many people came from Halifax to see, and I have been told that by request of the Halifax people the illumination was repeated on the following evening. Mr. Robert Dempster. and the late Mr. Joseph Beaumont were, I believe, chiefly instrumental in contriving and carrying out this scheme of decoration ; they were members of a Committee which was divided into sections, one part arranging the teas, another the music, &c.,-some of the other members of this Committee were my father, Mr. Edwin Thornton, and Mr. Thomas Hawley. The Savile Arms had "God bless the Prince of Wales" in gas along the front.

Some of the old people had tea in

a mill in Commercial Street. I remember
going in and seeing Miss Steele, who had
helped to prepare the room, sitting at the
head of one of the tables, and on the wall
behind her a trophy of Prince of Wales
feathers which she had made most
beautifully in white paper.

But life cannot be all sunshine and rejoicing
; besides these joyful occasions I remember
three public fasts ;-one for the Irish famine,
one for the rinderpest, and one when the
cholera was very terrible in England. Mr.
Atkinson used to say that the true way of
fasting was to see the things we liked, and to
abstain from them.

Of one event which happened in Church one
Sunday evening I heard much, though I was
not present. During the sermon when all was
quiet.

one of the clock-weights suddenly fell with a tremendous crash. One man was so terrified that he sprang up and rushed out of Church without his hat, never stopping until he reached his home across the Bridge. Some of the ladies ran to my father for protection, perhaps thinking. he would be able to help them in case of any Serious fracture or disablement, and one put her foot into his hat. The-weight fell once some time after, but that time my dear sister was the only person in the Church.

During the greater part of the time that Mr. Sandford held the living, my sister had charge ,of the choir, and used to write out the music for anthems, hymns, &c., and point the 'prayer-books, work which is not now necessary.

She also remained constant to her

Sunday-school teaching, and in 1867, the Teachers of the Girls' Sunday School gave me a handsome Bible, and my sister's class gave her a similar one.

When we had taught 50 years in the school, the Teachers, Elder Scholars and a few friends gave us a beautiful writing table, with its accompaniments, which was an immense surprise, as not a whisper of what was being done had reached our ears. All, or nearly all the subscribers came to see the table given, and Miss Musson made the presentation in a manner which reflected the pleasure of all, for, however undeserved we felt the gifts to be, it was a very great pleasure to have such a valuable token of the kind feeling of those amongst whom we had worked so long, and

some of whom we had known from babyhood.

I must not leave out of all mention our sorrows ; there were six of us children who grew up and the first to die was my eldest brother John; he was studying in London in order to be a doctor and I was living with him ; and then just before the examination of the College of Surgeons he died suddenly of epilepsy, in 1852. Between 1872 and 1876 the Angel of Death seemed to be resting with wings spread above our house; for my brother, the Rev. Samuel Collingwood Hamerton, fell asleep in 1872, in the Isle of Wight ; my brother Ernest, who was in practice with my father was taken from us in 1873 ; my mother in 1875 ; and my father, after a long life of eighty-two years, entered into rest in 1876 ; my youngest brother Joseph went to America, and died in 1881 at S. Elmo, Alabama. After my father's death my sister and myself removed to my present home which had been built for my brother Ernest some 15 years before, and there we lived together for twenty-three years, until in the autumn of 1899 she too, was called away-" not lost but gone before."

ELLAND CHURCH

Recollections! ah, how they come crowding into one's mind at the end of a long life! but here I find them gathering so constantly round the old Church and the Clergy and the Workers and the Services that this first chapter must be about our dear Parish Church of Elland. I remember it in 1826 and all the changes that have come since then; at that time its Chancel and Nave and Chapels were filled with pews of many sorts and fashions, square pews and oblong

Pews, pews lined with green, pews lined with crimson, pews curtained or partly curtained, but the two which appealed especially to us when children were the two church-wardens' pews which were opposite each other, just inside the Chancel, and were lined with scarlet, and had round them the staves of the different townships.

Galleries went nearly all round the Church, the Organ gallery being over the Chancel; this was the grandest, for on the front of it hung the King's Arms, and above the arch on either side were escutcheons of the Thornhill and Horton families; whilst above them, gradually decaying bit by bit, were several faded and torn regimental colours telling of brave men and stubborn fights, but looking to us only like queer dusty rags.

Besides the Organ Gallery there were also
the West Gallery under the Tower and the
South and North Galleries; all were
approached by mean wooden stairs, but the
North Gallery had an outside staircase; the
tower arch was partially filled with windows
of various shapes which helped to light the
West Gallery; the North Gallery was lighted
by large ordinary square skylights, such as
are need in houses, and also by small oblong
windows where the Clerestory would
have been had there been space.

In those days the East Window, which dates
from before the Reformation, was much
dilapidated; the lower lights had no coloured
glass in them, but were filled with plain
glass, which was hidden by a high painted
Reredos; the Reredos was surmounted by a
Cross, and on the Reredos was a painting of
an Altar with a

Lamb lying upon it; below, in the centre,
Were the Commandments in two divisions,
and on either side the Lord's Prayer and the
Creed. The most perfectly preserved part of
the East Window was the light representing
the Annunciation; and in the middle of the
window were the Arms of John of Gaunt.
Two large pictures hung one on either side
of the window, Moses on one side, Aaron on
the other, painted on wooden panels ; these
are now on the staircase walls of the
Rectory; they are not now paintings of any
intrinsic value and yet they have cost their
weight in gold; they became old and shabby,
being injured, it was said, at the funeral
service held in memory of the Princess
Charlotte, and the Churchwardens decided
to have them repainted; and when the Work
Was done they sent in a large bill to Rastrick
and to the other daughter parishes, claiming
that they ought to pay their

ELLAND CHURCH 1830

This page is Intentionally left blank

share; but they refused and this led to a long and expensive law-suit, which Elland lost.

The Pulpit of those days, a three-decker, had a handsome sounding-board with a solid dove on the top, and a painted one with outstretched wings underneath ; below the Pulpit was the Vicar's reading desk, and below that the Clerk's desk; and on the side of the Clerk's desk there was a curious contrivance :-the Choir and Organist sat in the East Gallery, and did not know before the service what Psalm or Hymn would be sung, or of What sort of measure therefore the tune had to be, so when the Clerk or the Vicar had chosen the Psalm or Hymn, the Clerk pulled out one of three " stops" at the side of his desk ; if he pulled out the top

one the Organist knew that the tune was to be in Long measure, if the second, in

Common measure, if the bottom one, Short measure, and at once gave instructions accordingly; the hymn book we used was Dr. Watt's, the psalms were the Old Version of Sternhold and Hopkins, and our great favourites wore the Hundredth and the Hundred-and-forth.

There were two vestries: a little wooden one where the' Organ now stands in which the clergyman used to change his surplice for the black gown which was used for preaching at that time, and an ugly building outside to the North-east of the Church which has been removed.

There were also two doors which have been built up; one at the North West corner of the Church leading to the Gallery, and in the stone above this door were the characters J.o.J.o. and at one time it was thought that they stood for 1010 and represented the date of the Church; this of course is not so as such a date would be in Roman numerals; moreover the Church in its oldest part appears to date from the transitional period between Norman and early English architecture; the other additional door was where the Hiley window is now, and opened from the outside vestry; and in this vestry there used to stand an oak table and four old "misereres."

Services were not held then in the evening, but on Sundays at 10-15 in the morning; and in the afternoon at 2-30, in the winter at 2; and on Wednesday and Friday mornings; so there was no need of much in the way of lights, but there used to be three Chandeliers in the Church; these were stolen about -A.D. 1830 and they were replaced by a much larger one ; it was only lighted when the Elland Society held their meetings in the Winter quarter and then the ladies of the congregation used to supply the wax candles for it, the only other light being supplied by candles in sockets fixed at the edges of the pews. This "Elland Society" is an evangelical society for helping young men who wish to be ordained to go to the' Universities ; as a rule the clergyman at Elland where the Society met was always admitted a member of the Society, but when the Rev. W. Atkinson was Incumbent they said he was a "Puseyite," (as he was,) blackballed him, and although he offered his room at the Parsonage for their use and the Church for their evening service as usual, they removed their place of meeting to Huddersfield and have never met at Elland since.

Outside there were several points of difference between the Church then and the Church now; the accompanying sketch shows the greatest of these ; the date on the clock in the original is 1809, .but the old picture itself from which the sketch is taken was painted about 1830. At that time there was a clock with only one face, the West door was blocked up, a wall, not railings, surrounded the Churchyard; there was a large gable in the south aisle and a long chimney at the east end of the Church. This long chimney belonged to a very little stove inside, and this very little stove was the only means provided for warming the Church-so it used to be very cold.

The Church-gates then were wooden and besides the gates there were two stiles, one on the South-west corner, the other at the North-east corner of the

Churchyard; just outside the gates were the old stocks, but more than sixty years ago they were removed to the outside of the Prison, and now are built into the adjoining wall. At the South-east corner of the Churchyard was a building which many people remember was called "Elland Castle;" this had been probably an Ecclesiastical building; and close by, just across Church street, or as it was then called Dog-lane, stood a barn, with a high-pitched roof and on its wall, looking West, a large wooden Cross, with the arm on one side somewhat fallen out of the straight line.

When I first remember the bells of Elland Church, they were a peal of six only, and those rather melancholy ones; but more than seventy years ago these were sent to Methley and were replaced

by the present peal of eight which cost about
,£550 and were first rung on March 13th,
1826.

Special times. and seasons used to be
marked by the ringing of certain bells ; for
example, at 8 o'clock on Sundays there was
always a bell, giving notice of service to be
held later on ; every night, and this custom
continued for some years after 1826 a
Curfew' was' rung at 8 o'clock; and a bell
was always rung on Shrove Tuesday and
was known as Pancake Bell.

Not very much was done in those ~ earlier
days in the way of decoration; but every
year on May the Twenty-ninth, the
anniversary of King Charles' escape in the
oak tree, the sexton mounted to the top of
the tower and there fixed a large branch of
oak ; and

at Christmas time he put branches of holly
on the galleries and sprays of holly in the
windows. No doubt decorations have
improved greatly since that day and the
crowds who come to a Harvest Festival and
admire the beautiful display of fruit and
flowers and wonder at the great loaves and
cabbages would have smiled with some little
contempt at those poor branches of holly but
I think that they carried a clearer message to
our hearts than any decorations however
beautiful can do to day simply because
Churches were decorated so seldom in those
days that we had not learned to criticise but
only to think of what the decorations meant.

The Sunday services were well attended and
for more than one reason; in the first place
the parish was of great extent, comprising
Greetland, West Vale

This page is Intentionally left blank

and Stainland; Rastrick did not contribute to
the size of the congregation
for, though part of the parish, it already had
its own Church; and in the second place as
will presently appear, there still remained a
certain amount of discipline.

The services being held at a quarter past ten
in the morning and at two in the afternoon, it
was the habit of the more distant and
wealthy parishioners to drive to Church for
the morning service, some putting up their
carriages at the Savile Arms; and after lunch
attending afternoon service and then driving
home in time for tea. One Of the people
Who used to drive to Church was Mrs.
Agnew, from Clayhouse ; her seat was the
top one in the West Gallery and to reach it
one had to pass between the two iron
standards which supported the curtains, and
I remember that her nieces, the Miss
Pollards, wore

such wide hats, that they were obliged to hold down the sides before they can get into the seat. The Chancel was occupied by the girls of the Sunday School, for we had a Sunday School even then ; the girls were taught in Mrs. Grace Ramsden's School and one of their teachers was Miss Tomazia Holroyd, of Stainland, who used to come every Sunday morning to teach, and was always at the School, ready, before nine o'clock. It was the family to which she belonged that presented the great silver Communion Flagon to the Church and the diamonds which are set in it belonged to Miss Tomazia ; the girls' school used to come into Church through the old vestry and the door where now is the Hiley window ; and they sat on forms, kept in order by a paid Dame. The boys sat under the West Gallery; they too had an officer of their own to keep them in order in Church, namely the Dog-whipper, a very important personage; his dress was not remarkable, but he had in his hand a cane, and often during service we heard the sound of the cane on the head of some unruly boy.

But we had two officers whose dresses were very beautiful, or at least remarkable, namely the Verger and the Organ-blower. The Verger had a coat and cocked hat edged with scarlet, scarlet plush waistcoat and scarlet plush breeches; his name was really Armitage but as sometimes happens he was very seldom called Armitage, and nearly always "Cabbage" and particularly "Old Cabbage." Our other beauty, the Organ-blower, was a man from the Elland Poor House, a building which may still be seen at the rope-walk ;'his attire was similar to that of the Verger except that his plush was yellow. Morning service

used to begin with a hymn, Bishop Kens
morning hymn "Awake my Soul;" and was
given out by the clerk who in sonorous voice
said "Let us sing to the Praise and Glory of
God the hymn Awake my Soul." At the
recitation of the Creed there was some
variety of ritual; some stood as before, a few
turned to the East, but the Sunday School
children turned round and faced their seats.
On the first Sunday of the month there was
Holy Communion and on those days the
Clergyman read the Gospel from the
Reading-desk and while he was doing so;
the Sexton advanced up the North Aisle,
bearing in his hands two great Pewter
Flagons, which he proceeded to place on the
Holy Table. My mother used to tell me that
on those days one or two Wesleyans also
used to come in from service at their
Meeting-house to receive Communion.
After the Nicene Creed, the Clergyman went
into the little wooden

vestry. took of his surplice and reappearing in his black gown, went up to the pulpit for the sermon; then he said a collect and began his sermon with the words--"The word of God, as it is written." I said that one cause that helped the good attendance at Sunday Services was the existence of discipline; this discipline was as follows: every Sunday when the congregation began to sing the Jubilate in Morning Service, the two Churchwardens solemnly left their pews and went out of the Church; they were going on their round and that was the round of the Public Houses ; from one to the other they went inspecting them, and where they found any loiterers, they haled them into Church; a very whole some discipline that might do some good at the present day.

The Evening Service, which began

with the hymn "From all who dwell below the skies," was little different from what it is now ; only after the first Lesson there was an interval, and this interval was the Organist's opportunity, for the congregation listened whilst he played a voluntary. The singing in Elland Church was hearty then as now, especially in the Te Deum, and it is worthy of note that in those days when Services as a rule had not very much brightness about them, the versicles and prayers were not said but monotoned.

At the Services on Wednesdays and Fridays the boys from the Free School and the girls from Mrs. Thornhill's Dame School came to Church; and after the opening of the National School on the last day of 1846, the scholars from that school came to Church also; on these days the Venite was sung, the singing being led by the schoolmaster; and further the children were catechised, a few at a time, standing in front of the reading desk.

These memories of Elland Church would be very far from complete, even as I remember them, unless something were added about the various restorations which the Church has undergone.

The work of Restoration was begun by the Rev. William Atkinson, in 1850, for in that year he raised the ringers' floor in the tower, and so brought the Whole of the west window into view; for until then the belfry floor had hidden the top of it. He had hoped to be able to carry out the whole of the Restoration but died before he could do more. Mr. Atkinson was succeeded by Mr. Meredith ; and the latter was preparing to carry on the work but the congregation disapproved of his plan, and he too died before the work was continued; and he was succeeded by Mr. Sandford, Who followed up the beginning made by Mr. Atkinson, With the Restoration of the Chancel, when Mr. Musson was his curate ; an important part of this work was the Restoration of the East Window to its present condition; and if that had been the only thing Mr. Sandford had ever done, he would have earned the gratitude of many generations, for the East Window is not the least of the glories of Elland Church; the arms of John of Gaunt had of course to be removed from their wrongful position in the centre of the window, and some other pieces of glass which had either never properly belonged to the window or could not be fitted in, but all these Were carefully preserved by Mr. Musson and may now be seen in the two small West Windows where their colour is still beautiful though

Facsimile of
an old
Picture of
Elland

This page is Intentionally left blank

their design is lost; at the same period the little old wooden vestry was removed, the old altar rails were used to rail off a Baptistery in the South West corner of the Church, and within them was placed a new Font; later, while Mr. Sandford was still incumbent, the Restoration of the Nave was carried out by Mr. Crossland, of Leeds, a pupil of Sir Gilbert Scott; and then the new Font was removed and the old one re-instated as being more in keeping with the architecture of the Church. Before the work of Restoration was begun the roof inside was hidden by plaster ceilings; but now all this was removed, and I well rem ember our excitement when the beautiful moulding round the Chancel Arch was first uncovered; I and my brother were then away in London, but our dear sister wrote to tell us about it; now, also, there was need of another vestry, as the wooden one was removed, and a most excellent altera-

tion was made in procuring it; under the
Sanctuary is a chamber which used always
to be known as the Bone House-and with
good reason too for it was the place where
the Sexton kept his tools, and he was in the
habit of putting there any loose bones that he
might find when digging graves; one very
early memory I have of that chamber, for
when I was still a very little child my nurse
took me there to see the body of a poor little
baby that had been found drowned in the
river, well, at the time of Restoration, they
discovered that there was a staircase leading
from the Bone House up to the Sanctuary, so
the place was cleansed and became the
vestry, and was used as such until the
present one was built in 1879, in memory of
Dame Savile.

The other stained-glass windows are of
modern date; the West window was

made by Wailes of Newcastle, and given by the friends of Christopher and William Atkinson, father and son, who were successively incumbents of Elland from 1800 to 1850. The Hiley window and the Transfiguration, which was given by Mr. Holdsworth, of Halifax, are both by Hardman; those in memory of the Thwaite family and of John Wilkinson, are by Powell of Leeds; 'the one in memory of Mr. and Mrs. Musson is by Kemp; but the artists of the Rawson and Hirst windows are not known.

Besides services in the Parish Church in old days, there were cottage lectures held on week-days at Elland Edge, and at the outlying district of Raw Royds, and also in Mrs. Grace Ramsden's schools. At Stainland the Church was originally a Chapel, and was converted into a Church in 1841 and consecrated, at which service the sermon was preached by Mr. Christopher Atkinson from the text, " My son, give me thy heart." Greetland Church was built during the incumbency of Mr. Sandford, and part of the funds were raised by a large Bazaar in the National Schools; and lastly, West Vale Church was built while Mr. Musson was rector, and a little later that part of the parish was separated from Elland.

RESTORATION OF THE CHURCH.

I HAVE told some of my memories of Elland Church, but it will be best to refer for particulars to the newspapers of the time; we were always careful to preserve such cuttings from papers as were likely to be valuable, and they contain much information which would be otherwise very difficult, or even impossible to obtain.

All the pews in the Church were of deal except the one in which we sat-lt was of oak, and had been the pew of my great-great-uncle, Captain Northend Nicholls, and was very old, for the door bore the date 1690, and it had a brass plate with his name upon it. The reason of its remaining, when all the other old oak pews gave place to later deal ones, was that when the change was made Captain Nicholls went down to the Church, and, standing before his pew with his sword drawn, dared anyone to touch it ; so it was left there until in later days the Church was restored, and the last oak pew vanished together with the deal ones.

When we began going to Church my mother expected us to behave very well, and punished us if we did not; indeed, the last whipping I remember was for this very thing ; my brother and my sister and I had been naughty in Church, and my mother had seen us, and we knew what to expect when we reached home; I was then seven years' old, and I remember hoping, as we walked through the church-yard, that she would forget-but she did'nt.

The order in which the successive restorations were carried out will be seen by the following note, kindly written for me by Miss Sandford, the daughter of one of our former rectors:

"In 1853 the new organ was placed on the ground floor, and a new pulpit and reading-desk were erected ; considerable alterations were made in the Chancel in 1856 and at the West end, including the restoration of the old East window; in 1859 the illuminated clock was placed in the tower, and the tower itself Wes restored; in 1865-6 the North-west and South galleries were re-moved, and the painted deal pews replaced with oak stalls."

But the Restoration came too late to save some things; I do not remember them, but my dear mother used to tell me of the quaint figures on the monuments in the Chancel in older days; where they went to I do not know, but the memory of them has been preserved by Mr. John Watson, in his History of Halifax, and we borrow from him the following account of them :

"In a part belonging to Savile and Thornhill, a man kneeling at prayer, and in armour, his upper garment alternately white and red, behind him, in the same posture, his wife, her garment the same, only in two places thereof appear two bars gemells, argent; behind her, another woman, in the same posture and dress. Under these figures, in old characters : " Orate pro prosperitate Willielmi Thornhill et Elzizabet uxoris ejus et johannes (sic) Thornhill, filii et heredis eorundem, et Jhnae uxoris suae, et prosperitate Nichi . . et Agnetis consortis suae, filioirum et filiarum eorundem, ac ominium Benefactorium suorum." [Pray for the welfare of William Thornhill and Elizabeth his wife and John Thornhill, their son and heir and Joanna his wife and for the welfare of Nich(olas) and Agnes his wife, of their sons and daughters and of all their benefactors.] With the above were also the figures of a man in armour, kneeling, behind him his wife and three children."

"in the North Quire, the figure of the greatest part of a woman, in a praying posture, and four children below, also praying; over the children's heads the names Elezabeth, Mary, Jane, Dorithy. Inscription round the stone: " Here slepeth the body of Francis, daughter' of Godfrey Boswell, Esq., wife of John Savile, of Newhall, Esq., whose soul returned to God that gave it, February 26, 1609.

The accompanying illustration is copied from a plate in the same History of Halifax.

The following are extracts from the Halifax Guardian, giving particulars of the work of Restoration between the years 1856 and 1866:

" A handsomely stained window by Mr. Wailes, of Newcastle, has been placed in the tower light of Elland Church, as a monument to the Revs. Christopher and William Atkinson, father and son, who, for a period of 47 years were successively incumbents of Elland . . . We give the inscription which is inserted in two lines at the foot of the window in church text: " In memory of the Rev. C. Atkinson, M.A., incumbent of Elland for 4: years; also of the Rev. W. Atkinson, M.A., his son and successor, who faithfully filled his place for six years. This window has been erected in grateful remembrance by their parishioners and friends." It seems a pity that so handsome a window should be hid by the unsightly gallery which stands in front of it, and we hope to see the day when the good taste of the inhabitants will again display itself by removing this and the one at the East end, if not all the galleries."

ELLAND CHURCH.--"We have already noticed the judicious and spirited manner in which the restoration of the East end of this ancient and beautiful Church was commenced, and has been carried on. We are now happy to report the completion of the excellent work, in the erection of suitable oak reredos, side screens, and communion rails, and the restoration of the beautiful East window. The wood work, which has been designed by J. A. Cary, Esq., of Durham, and executed by J. Moody, of the same city, is elaborate, yet so designed as thoroughly to harmonize with the fabric in its age and general character. The reredos and side screens are divided by buttressed stiles into arched compartments filled in the beads

with beautiful tracery. In the panels of the
reredos the Ten Commandments are carved in
raised letters cut out in the solid wood. The side
screen on the South is advanced in order to leave
room behind for an entrance from the vestry
below, thus restoring the old practice of this
Church; and in the two panels nearest the
communion rails are recessed arches for sedilia
or seats for the officiating clergy. The whole
screen is surmounted by a richly carved
strawberry leaf moulding. The communion
railing is supported by stiles, the squares
between which are filled in with exquisite
perforated tracery work, describing cusped
circles intricately interwoven after the richest
examples of perforated G0thic work. The whole
carving is beautifully executed, and is a model
of correct and artistic workmanship. The old
East window, it will be remembered, contained
mutilated remnants of subjects and stories,
which showed that this window had once been a
gem of art in glass staining. An examination of
the fragments proved that (at least in the Elland
window) the old glass stainers were no mean
artists ; and that it is vulgar calumny to accuse
them of bad drawing, and deficient perspective.
The committee under whom

the work of restoration has been carried on wisely entrusted to Mr. Wailes, of Newcastle, the task of restoring I window which, though it had been so sadly mutilated, contained many a quaint and lovely torso of antique art. That eminent artist undertook the work with a feeling kindred to that which has dictated the entire restoration; and the result is a window which is probably unequalled in beauty in the North of England. Quiet and unobtrusive, its beauties will reward the most minute and critical attention. Brilliant in colours where brilliancy is required, the effect is so beautifully subdued and toned that all may look on the window with pleasure, and the tasteful must examine it with growing admiration. There is none of that unsightly glare which too often characterises modern stained windows; no patches of primitive colours scattered with kaleidosc0pe-like effect; no masses of crude colouring laid on, as it would seem in some windows, with a besom for a brush. The faces and hands are drawn with minutest care ; the draperies diapered ; the very floor and background filled with exquisite work. In fact all, who wish to see what a good East window ought to be,

will do well to go to Elland Church, and see
what the East window there is. We hope that a
sufficient amount will be realised by the
collections to-morrow, and at the Bazaar which
will be held on Thursday and Friday next, to
make up the deficiency existing betwixt the
contributions already received and the expenses
unavoidably incurred in carrying out a
restoration upon which we beg to congratulate
the churchmen and inhabitants of Elland."

RESTORATION OF ELLAND' CHURCH.---"
On Sunday, as announced in our last, collections
were made in the afternoon and evening, in aid
of the Restoration Fund. In the afternoon prayers
were read, and the sermon preached by the Rev.
F. Musson, whose text was, I Chronicles xiv.,
19. In the evening, the Rev. Mr. Oakes read
prayers, and the Rev. E. Sandford preached from
Psalm xxvi., 8. The choir was strengthened by
Miss Tankard and Messrs. Priestley, Baume, and
Carter, of the Parish Church choir. The services
were Bridgewater's, and the anthems Webb's
"Thou Lord," and " The Lord is the portion of
the just." On Thursday, the Sale of Work in
furtherance of the Restoration Fund commenced in the National Schoolroom, Elland,

which was very tastefully decorated, the walls being draped in white and pink, with festoons of evergreens. The tables were arranged all-round the room, and were amply supplied with useful, ornamental, and fancy articles. Exotic flowers in vases adorned the tables, and several singing birds were hung in the room. A quadrille band enlivened the proceedings, and the attendance was large and fashionable. On the first day the proceeds of the sales (including a donation of £5 from Mrs. Edwards, and of £5 from Mrs. Akroyd) amounted to £146. Yesterday, about £50 more 'was realised ; and, as a considerable quantity of articles remain on hand, the sale will be continued this day from two to six o'clock. The ladies who preside at the stalls are Mrs. Bury and Mrs. W. Slater (who preside at the refreshment stall), Mrs. Sandford, Mrs. Tomlin, and Mrs. Wilkinson, and Misses Armitage, M. Atkinson, Byrne, Crowley, Hamerton, Hollinshead, Hope, Musson, Outram. Pitchforth, and Scholefield."

From this it will be seen that by the time Bazaars had begun here. and though we did not try then to raise by them the immense sums which we raise now-a-days, we worked very hard for them and they provided substantial help to the funds.

RE-OPENING 0F ELLAND CHURCH.---" This ancient Church, first, erected about the year 1080, and afterwards enlarged about the middle of the fourteenth century, has been undergoing a very judicious Restoration during the last few months. Externally, as well as internally a most striking improvement has been effected. From a mutilated and dilapidated edifice this ancient place of worship has become, through skilful management, one of the most beautiful and interesting of our Yorkshire Churches. The large and disproportioned gable, with its square mullioned lights, which recently formed the striking disfigurement of the southern side of the Church has disappeared, and the aisle on which it stood, has been restored to its original proportions. Square headed windows, in the decorated style, and corresponding with the ancient ones still remaining, have been erected in lieu of the barbarous creations of later times. The unsightly dormer lights and the rudely constructed clerestory windows intended to give light to the galleries within. have bun removed. and the original character o! the sacred edifice restored. An excellent view of the whole is obtained from the north east side of the churchyard. Here, the view comprises the Church with its chancel and north aisle seen in perspective; and the beautifully proportioned tower, with its battlements rising above the surrounding houses, the background being formed by the quaint gables and mullioned windows of the Rose and Crown Inn. Internally the work of Restoration has been carried on with reverential care, and the success which has attended it is universally remarked. The ponderous galleries erected during the 17th and 18th centuries, in the north and south aisles, and in the tower and across the chancel, have been taken down, and the aisle roofs re-constructed in massive oak, with carved corbels in stone. The ancient roof of the nave has also been exposed to view. The huge pillars of the tower are seen in all the breadth of their massive proportions, and in the impressive severity of their style. The entire nave and chancel are viewed from east to west without obstruction; and, midway, the great central arch marks the ancient division of the

HOUSES AT THE TOP of CHURCH-STREET

This page is Intentionally left blank

chancel from the nave. This interesting feature of the Church is a pointed arch of transitional Norman character, with double cone and roll mouldings. The north aisle is open through its entire length, and the chapel of St. Nicholas at its eastern extremity, with its curious monuments, is exposed to view. Here the ancient families of Savile and Thornhill founded a chantry and service and erected their memorial windows, in which they besought the prayers of the people for their "gude prosperity, mercy, and grace." In this aisle a new stained window has been placed, "In affectionate memory of the late Abram Hirst, of Hullen Edge, Esq., by his nephews and nieces, A.D. 1866." The subject is the "Good Samaritan." In the south aisle the vista is obstructed by the organ, which is placed at its east end, in the chapel of St. John the Baptist. This chapel was founded for a chantry and service, by Sir John Savile, Knight, and Isabel, his wife, " for a chaplain to celebrate therein for the good estate of John, Duke of Acquitain and Lancaster, of John Savile, Knight, and Isabel, his wife, and the children of the said John and Isabel and for the souls of the said Duke and said John and Isabel and the souls of their children after death; and for the souls of Henry, late Earl of Lancaster, of John Sayvill. Knight, and Margery, his wife, parents of said John Sayvill, Knight ; also of Thomas de Bland and Joan, his wife, parents of the said Isabel, of John Rylay, Thomas Cross, chaplain, and Richard Schepard, of Eland, and the friends and benefactors of said John Sayvill, Knight, and Isabel, and for the souls of all the faithful departed."

At the west end of the south aisle the ancient font, after having been completely renovated, is once more employed for its original purpose. The floor of the Church has been laid with encaustic tiles of appropriate character, and the interior lighted by gas standards, in brass, and of beautiful design. In the chancel a window has been erected by Edward Rawson, Esq., which adds to the " dim religious light " of St. Mary's quire. These, with the addition of considerable alterations in the roof of the chancel internally, and of the whole building externally, complete the work of renovation, and have rendered the building an honour to the parish and to the gentlemen by whose exertions and enterprise it has been accomplished. Amongst the most active members of the working committee appointed to raise the funds and superintend the Restoration, special mention must be made of the following gentlemen, viz. :Mr. Thomas W. Townsend, Mr. G. R.

Robinson, churchwardens, the Rev. E. Sandford, the incumbent, Mr. J. Wilkinson, Mr. J. Hamerton, Mr. R. Walker and Mr. John Crossley. The work of Restoration was entrusted to Mr. Crossland, of Leeds, architect. The builders employed to execute the work were, for the joinery, Mr. Henry Hawkyard, and for the stone masonry, Messrs. Hanson Brothers, all of this place. The Church is now calculated to accommodate nearly eight hundred persons, the whole being free seats. The total cost of the alterations is estimated at about £1, 500, and of that sum £1,150 has already been subscribed. It is not anticipated that there will be any difficulty in raising the comparatively small balance. From an early hour in the morning the excellent bells rang merry peals, and sounded the glad tidings of completion far away over the hills and valleys surrounding Elland. A large royal standard hoisted high on the battlements also pointed out the whereabouts of the Church itself to the stranger visitors. Shortly before eleven o'clock, the appointed time for the service to commence, all hands appeared simultaneously to cease from labour, and the whole neighbourhood, including the wealthy employer, the skilful artizan, and the indigent poor, wended their way to the spot, where in one common cause, and for one common purpose, no distinctions may exist beyond those of virtue and goodness alone. The Church was re-opened by the Bishop of Ripon. The morning service was conducted by the Incumbent and the communion service by the Lord Bishop, assisted by the Venerable Archdeacon Musgrave. After the service his lordship ascended the pulpit and preached an eloquent and impressive sermon from the 24th and 25th verses of the Epistle of St. Jude, at the conclusion of which he said that he could not retire without giving expression to his unfeigned thankfulness at what had been done within that building since he had last the privilege of standing in it. The great liberality the parishioners had shown in restoring the Church of God and investing it with almost the freshness of youth, but still retaining all its old associations, was most satisfactory and encouraging. The place in which their fathers and their forefathers had worshipped God, and where many souls had been trained for the temple above, had now been placed

in a condition which befitted its sacred name,
and he trusted that those who came hither to
worship in the future would come with pure
hearts and souls, and would worship according
to the established Liturgy of the Church. There
was still, it appeared, a debt upon the building.
The whole cost of Restoration he understood to
be £ 1,500; of that sum £350 remained to be
contributed. He felt, however, that he had but to
ask the people who congregated within its walls
to be forward in completing that which they had
so well begun, and as they had displayed so
much liberality already he would urge upon
them not to let it be said that a single fraction of
debt remained upon it, but let it be in this respect
also worthy of the worship of God. The
collections amounted to about £80."

The date here suggested for the building of
the Church, A.D. 1080, must not be
supposed to be the date of any part of the
existing structure, for the oldest part seems
to be the chancel arch, and an eminent
architect places its date confidently as
between A.D. 1180 and A.D. 1200.

Also one is not quite so sure now that it was altogether a good thing to remove the large and disproportioned gable from the South aisle, for at least it served to mark part of the history of the building and also admitted much needed light.

It was difficult even then to raise the large sums of money Which were required, but perhaps not so difficult as now-a-days; and I remember that we raised, in the Christmas tide of 1857, more than £60 by a great Christmas tree, which was shown for two days in the school.

Danesbury House, Timber Street Elland.
Pulled down in 1881.

This page is Intentionally left blank

ELLAND TOWN

No one who knows Elland now, with its many streets of small houses, its "monuments of industry" in the shape of long chimneys, and its smoke-laden

atmosphere, can at all imagine what the place was like three or four hundred years ago, when one of the Elands could write to a friend in London, and promise him, if he would come to this little Yorkshire town, "the best hunting, deer-stalking, and salmon fishing of the N orth." The Calder was in those days a clear stream, as indeed it was in much later times, for a few years ago a man told me that he could remember catching trout there six inches long, and as children we used to fish with our hands in the shallows, and catch dace, loaches, and gudgeon. In 1776 the Rev. Thomas Twining visited Elland, and though he does not praise the town. he does praise very highly the lovely scenery around.

He says :

" You descend to Eiland by a hill monstrously long. and very steep, which we walked down. The view from this hill was the finest I had seen of the extensive kind, the Calder winding its way through the meadows below the town, high hills covered with thicker, closer, and larger woods than I saw anywhere else. I thought this was all I had to see, and that nothing would do after it. After we had put up our horses, and ordered dinner at Elland, we walked through the town. which is dirty, and promises nothing, to the turnpike road at one end of it (I forget whither the road leads). when you come suddenly upon the view I told you of, and which is far beyond anything that my scanty travels have shown me. You see partly the same objects which you saw from the hill above the town; but everything is nearer, more distinct. compact, and picturesque: and the great beauty of all (and which I think essential to a first-rate view) is, that you look down directly upon it, and it begins from the feet of the spectator; a circumstance out of the reach of painting, and only to be found in God's landscapes! You stand upon the road; over your head are high cliffs, on the top of which is a footpath; directly under you another road; under that, the river winding along through green meadows, with a fall or two that have more effect to the ear than the eye; to the right, on the side you stand on, the Church and town hanging upon the hill, with cottages, &c., quite down to the water's side ; the bridge, beyond it the river losing itself among woody hills, the valley opening to a distant view, where you catch a last glimmer of the river before it finally departs. To the left the river, after a long winding, loses itself (nearer to the eye) by turning to the right among high hills richly covered with woods, the rock in some places peeping through them. These woods extend on the opposite side of the river both ways as far as you can see, only a beautiful green rim of meadow between them and the river. Immediately under the wood is a path that accompanies the river as far as you can see to the left,

and must be the most delicious of all walks.
Imagine all the living accompaniment. to this
scene ; cattle feeding in the meadows. boys
bathing, people on foot and on horseback,
above, below, over your head, and under your
feet. After dining in a charming cellar-like room
at the Savile Arms (the whole place and its
environs are Sir George Savile's), made on
purpose to cool heated travellers, we had a mind
to see the view again from the highest path,
which was over our heads; but, time as it was,
we agreed that the road below was the best spot;
above, the view becomes more distant, greater,
but less beautiful and piquant. We could
discover Halifax from this height; indeed, it is
but a few miles from Elland; the valley through
which the river winds to your left hand leads to
it, and is all in the same beautiful style. And so,
farewell Elland; if I forget thee, let my right
hand forget her cunning ! "

Again, writing of a visit in 1781, he says :

" The whole ride from Huddersfield is a
climax of rich and beautiful country. There is a
new road made from Huddersfield to Ealand,
along the side of the Calder, by which many

terrible tugs over the hills are avoided ; and you are well paid for the loss of some great staring prospects by the nearer, more distinct, and picturesque views of the lower road. This is-great part of it---cut through a thick wood hanging down to the river, which you see glittering through the boughs under you on your left, a woody and rocky steep rising on your right, the little falls in the river producing a perpetual rustle of water, and the effects of the whole varying at every bend of the road. There is still '21 considerable descent to Ealand, and a magnificent view. The weather was cloudy and unsettled ; just as the view opened it began to rain. The little I could look at, with the head of the chaise in my way, was veiled in mist. I murmured sadly; it answered, for the rain stopped. A little gleam of sunshine, through an opening cloud at the extremity of a long vale on the left, came stealing along, till by slow degrees the whole valley and the town were illuminated, part of the distant hills still remaining in shade and forming a sort of black frame to this bright and beautiful picture. I never felt anything so fine. I shall remember it, and thank God for it, as long as I live. I I am sorry I did not think to say grace after it. Are we to be grateful for nothing

but beef and pudding?---to thank God for life,
and not for happiness?"

The " thicker, closer, and larger woods " are
now rapidly disappearing, the very hills
themselves are in some places being cut
away, while the spirit of the river, were it
conscious of its blackness, might well be
supposed to bemoan its fate, as is epresented
in the following verses, written long ago by
my dear brother, S. C. Hamerton :

THE LAMENT OF FATHER CALDER.

MIDNIGHT, with one pale star upon her brow
Stole up the valley, as with strange unrest
Gave forth a murmur, faint and sad and low,
Dark Calder's turbid breast.

Was it that evermore his prattling stream
In mazy circlets 'mid the pebbles played?
Or that the night wind, like some soothing
dream
Crept through the tangled glade?

O no! there was a something in that sound,
That while it awed me, bade me linger there,
A something-as when dreamland forms
surround
At eve, the old man's chair.

As thus I listened, motionless and still,
Striving in vain to pierce the deepening shade,
The silver Queen of Night clomb o'er the hill,
And lent me kindly aid.

For cowering on the river bank I spied
An aged form that, with dishevelled hair
Veiling its features, strove in vain to hide
The depth of its despair.

And yet I knew that tho' in mortal guise
It was no mortal, such a sudden awe
Crept o'er me as, all speechless with surprise,
That old-world shape I saw.

Nor unperceived my presence: straight it rose,
Cast back its dripping locks, and hated a face
Whereon was written care without repose,
Indelible disgrace.

Then with a voice so soft and musical
It told its sorrows to my willing ears,
That not the hardest heart had checked the fall
Of sympathetic tears.

It told me of a loathsome prison den,
And how each year one night's repose was given
Whereon to tell his woes, and breathe again
The pure soft air of heaven.

Far down beneath the wave that prison lay,
'Neath the weird regions where the mermen
dwell,
Its dark recesses nor the light of day,
Nor the sound of village bell

Had ever reached ;-naught but the ceaseless flow
Of surging waters with the same sad moan
Forever journeying overhead-below
Some prisoned comrade's groan.

Why reft from him the realms he swayed of old,
What day would bring a respite from his woes;
All this he told me, but, or ere he told
Forbad me to disclose.

" In days of old, with pomp and royal state
'Twas mine to rule where now, alas! I dwell
A hopeless prisoner, with the darkest fate
That ever King befell."

Thus spake he, and anon his quivering eye
Waxed bolder, as the days of ancient might
Rose up again before his memory
In vision clear and bright.

Then, with a gleam of re-awakening pride,
He told, in accents fitting to his dream.
Tales of the by-gone, ere pollution dyed
Old England's fairest stream.

71 Elland Town

How in those kindlier times with gentle sway
Ruled Father Calder, as with footstep free
His crystal stream throughout the livelong day
Danced onward joyously.

Onward thro' tangled copse and lonely vale,
Past beetling crag, and over-hanging tree,
Whose guardian branches, with a sweet sad wail,
Bent o'er him lovingly.

But chiefly how he loved to linger near
A tiny hamlet, nestling on the brow,
Of one steep bank there, as he paused to hear
A music soft and low

From out the guardian of that lovely spot,
The massy tower that, giant-like and grim,
Kept watch o'er many a tiny sleeping cot,
Down to the water's brim * * * *

Sudden he ceased, and with a piercing cry
Plunged 'neath the surges, for returning day
Darting her first faint beams athwart the sky
Had summoned him away.

Even in 1829 Elland was a quaint village; it
had three drapers' shops, one jeweller's
shop, and one toy shop, with very common
toys. Miss Swan, who was a

niece of my grandmother, and a very little woman, once wished to buy some toys for us, and asked the toy shop keeper if he had no better toys-no London toys? His answer was: "I don't know who you are-you're a very little woman, but a very great dame ! " There was no book-seller's shop, but, I am sorry to say. there was a pawnshop; we may indeed be thankful that Elland has so far advanced as to banish the three golden balls from its streets There was no professional confectioner, but many of the cottagers sold bread, large thin-cakes, which were put on end in the windows, and parkin.

There were not more than three mills in Elland at that time; the chief industry was hand-loom weaving in the cottages, the looms being upstairs, and the women usually winding downstairs. At most of the cottage doors you would see

SOUTH HOUSE
NOW THE
COUNCIL OFFICE

This page is Intentionally left blank

women or children "setting cards"; fifteen hundred of the little teeth had to be put into a pierced strip of leather for a halfpenny. Oatbread or "havercake" baking was another occupation ; it was done in the cottages on "bakestones" on which the mixed meal and water was thrown with a little wooden shovel, called a " baking spittal." I have heard that when the recruiting sergeant of the Duke of Wellington's Regiment, known as the "Havercake Lads," went seeking recruits, he always carried a "havercake" on the point of his bayonet.

There were not many streets in Elland in 1829; the principal ones were Watergate (now called Northgate). South End (Southgate), Dog Lane (Eastgate), Westgate, and Castlegate. Saddleworth Road was called "The Bank." There were also New Street, (built in .My great great uncle, Captain Nicholl's time) and

Timber Street. In most of the streets were barns with high-pitched roofs, and grand old houses, (especially one beautiful gabled house opposite the prison), besides cottages-one in particular I remember in Westgate, with a door heavily studded with nails, and a curious wooden appendage to fasten it.

Elland was plentifully supplied with water by wells---those called the Town Wells were opposite the Old Prison, and were four in number, close together, but I can only remember two being used, as the water in the others was not clear From these the women or boys (seldom or never the men) carried the household supply of water in large tin cans on their heads, a small round cushion being placed under the can. A flat wall surrounded the wells on three sides, and on this the women rested their cans, while indulging in the gossip which made the well almost as

interesting a place as "the mangle" indeed.
when the wells were done away with, old
people were heard to say that when the
custom of carrying the weekly wash to one
common mangle for the necessary
smoothing should also die out, they would
"nivver know nowt!" Behind the wells was a
green field, and also the beautiful old house
which I mentioned before; there was also a
well at the Bridge End, and draw-wells in
New Street and Westgate, and no doubt in
other places. The "Spa Well" at the bottom
of the Upper Edge, not far from South End,
was so called because it contained
chalybeate water: people have indeed
suggested formerly that if properly
managed, Elland might be made famous for
its medicinal water, and so become another
Cheltenham or Leamington, and, old
inhabitants of Elland may perhaps be
pardoned for thinking, a very much prettier
one. The

" Canker-Dyke " though quite clear, was always coloured with chalybeate, and there used to be a bridge over it in Dog Lane, not far from Marshall Hall.

The Halifax Road was then in parts quite an avenue; a toll-bar at Salterhebble was said to be just a mile from Elland. Toll-bars abounded; there was one at the top of Elland, and another at the further end of the Long Walk called the "Little Nan Bar"; another on the Brighouse Road, one on the rise of the hill going up the Fixby Road (now called Dewsbury Road), one down Dog Lane, and another at South End. At these toll gates a penny or two-pence was demanded from riding or driving passengers, and a half-penny from all foot passengers at a toll-bar on the road from Halifax to North Dean, which in consequence is still known locally as "Ha'-penny Bar."

One peculiar and beautiful feature of Elland
was, and is, the three roads one above
another; Saddleworth Road, on the Bank,
Long Wall, and the Nab, now called Hullen
Edge Road. It was from the centre one of
these, Long Walk, that Mr. Twining saw the
view he most admired, and though man has
done 'much to take away its beauty it is still
a glorious scene. In my younger days there
were no mills or houses along the lower
road, and the field between this and the river
was called "Pike Purse." For some way
along this road there were posts and chains
on the side nearest the river as a protection
from the water, but further on, past the malt-
kiln, the causeway was on the top of the
wall, as also on the road above, or "Long
Wall." In spite of the apparent danger,
accidents were uncommon; a waggon once
went over, the driver not being sober, and on
another occasion a woman walking in

pattens fell over and broke her leg.

The Wood above the Halifax Road, now
known as "Elland Wood," was then called
the "Hall Wood"; there a few Lent lillies and
lillies of the valley might be found, and
once, walking on the Halifax Road, just
within the wood, I found a root of
moonwort. The Park Wood, which still
keeps its old name, was beautiful in spring
and early summer with primroses, beds of
woodruff, and forget-me-nots, and both that
and the Hall Wood were at the proper
season, carpeted with wild hyacinth.
Between thirty and forty years ago the Park
Wood was preserved, and if you walked
through you might hear the call of the
pheasant, and see the rabbits scuttling right
and left. Between Blackley and the Ainleys
was a small wood in the shape of the letter
P, called therefore P Wood, and the Ainley
Wood; between the Upper and

Lower Edges was a small plantation, and beyond the Lower Edge, on the slope of the hill above the Calder. Strangstrye Wood, which still remains, and the top of which bears the name of Harrycastle Hill. What is now Victoria Road was then a lane, called Town Field Lane; it was a kind of private road, and to show this, was closed one day in the year. I have been told that funerals passing up New Street to go through Town Field Lane to Blackley graveyard, had to leave some small article ---as a glove or handkerchief-behind as a toll, or acknowledgment, receiving it back on their return. The only buildings in South Lane were one or two cottages, and the "Woodman," which house had quite an avenue leading to it. Elland has always grown famous fruit and vegetables; in the garden of one of the cottages in South Lane grew most beautiful Magnum Bonum Plums, while at Whitwell Place,

Peaches, nectarines, and Orleans plums,
were grown in the open air.
wall rule fern (asplenium ruta muravia) grew
on Elland bridge, and outside the walls of
the Bank House and we once found wall
spleenwort (asplenium trichomanes), and
black spleenwort (asplenium adiantum
nigrum) to two walls near Elland. The
northern hard fern (bleochnum boreale)
could be found in plenty on the rocks at Nab
End, and when my father went his rounds he
seldom came home without plants of
flowers.

In my mother's time a little Grebe or
Dabchick used to come up to the river as far
as Elland Bridge and in 1847 a Nightingale
came to Ainley Wood and sang gloriously ;
people in new Street said they could hear it
easily in the early mornings; and indeed, so
many went to hear it that they drove it away.

Elland
A.D. 1830

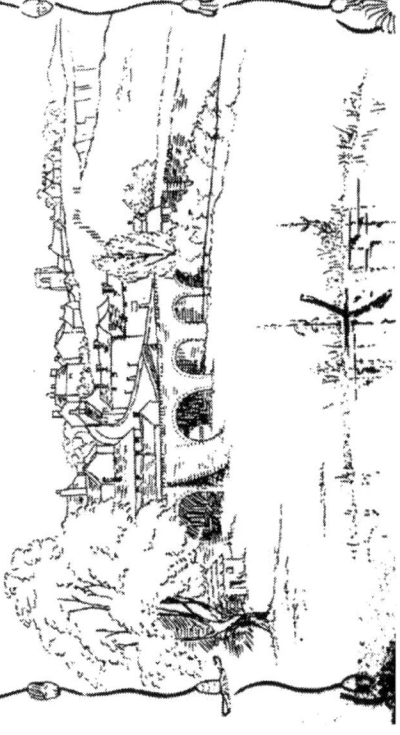

WHITWELL PLACE

Before the Dene Head Reservoir was made,
we had frequent foods, in which the river
sometimes rose very rapidly. Once when my
father had appointed to meet my cousin at
the stepping stones below Ash Grove, he
found, when he crossed the bridge, that the
river had risen so much that he grew
somewhat alarmed as to my cousin's safety;
however, he was at the meeting place, but
had had to wade across the river knee-deep.
Another time the same cousin was nearly.
lost in a snowdrift on the hill above
Blackley, where he and his horse were for
some hours almost buried and unable to
move: just as the groom was about to be sent
in search of him he arrived home, safe, but
wet through and quite exhausted.

Before the National Schools were built there
was Mrs. Grace Ramsden's School, behind
the Church. always known

as the "Back O' th' Church School," and the scholars were called "Back O' th' Church Dumplings." There was also Mrs. Thornhill's Charity School; the children attending this school had given to them every year the material for undergarments, which they were taught to make for themselves, and for grey stockings, Which they learnt to knit; cottage bonnets, trimmed with a ribbon laid straight across, sometimes blue, sometimes violet, sometimes green; a green cotton dress, made With short sleeves, a white muslin tippet,' a checked apron, and one shoe, the parents being expected to buy the other, and the children always came to Church in their new clothes for the first time on Trinity Sunday.

The Lord Wharton Bibles have been given ever since I can remember; they were, in my earliest recollections, bound in good brown binding with brass clasps.

and. I believe, either "The Whole Duty of Man," or a " Companion to the Altar," was often given with them.

The National Schools were built by subscription, and were opened in the year 1846. The Opening was celebrated by the performance of a grand Oratorio, which (Christy Minstrels and Variety Entertainments were not then known in Elland) realised the sum of £50 for the building fund. Bazaars were not then the inevitable things they have since become, so we had no bazaar, nor even any tea parties for the schools, but a few of us sewed quietly at home, and filled a large basket with plain and fancy work, which basket was sent round to various people, who might select purchases from it, and the money raised by this means was about another £25. When the National Schools were first used, the boys were taught downstairs, the girls upstairs, and at the west end of the school was the schoolmaster's house. with a pretty little garden. The upper part of this house was afterwards made into a class-room for the infants, which was chiefly filled by a sloping gallery rising in rows of seats from the floor to the middle of the-window. There was also the private school taught for so many years by Miss Steele; how many people of Elland and its outskirts received their education from her one scarcely dare begin to calculate; it is not often that three generations have learnt under one teacher, as has been the case with her.

As the town grew, fresh accommodation was required for school children, and in 1871 the National School proved too small for the number of scholars; so, wishing to show my father some token of gratitude, the people of Elland built the

Elland
National Schools

This page is Intentionally left blank

Boys' School, at a cost of £900 as a testimonial to him.

The Post Office, in modern town: so important a place, was in old Elland very primitive indeed. My first recollections of it are when it was at the place now called the Old Post Office, which also gave its name to Post Office Yard, but I am told that in still earlier days it was on the opposite side of the street. The Post Office of my childish memories was attached to a little shop, a real general dealer's: here could be bought all kinds of things, from vegetables to valentines (perhaps if there were any specialities in most Elland eyes they were yeast, liquorice root, and " scaarin stooan"), but what we most enjoyed buying were Christmas hymns at a half penny each, which were a great delight. They consisted of a single sheet of very thin paper, having a small picture of the Nativity at the top, and an ornamental border all round. Ten 11):an were on this sheet, "Christians, awake" and "While shepherds' watched" being those now best known. The Post Office was kept by two old women, Tet, and Hannah Buckley; Tet was postmistress, and Hannah used'. at one time to deliver the letters, carrying them in her apron. Getting a post office order was then a work of time; we usually went and stated our requirements and then retired for half-an hour's conversation with a friend until the great business of preparation was complete and our post office order ready. The railway was opened about 1842, and for some time the accommodation was very scanty. Third-class passengers had to travel in carriages like cattle trucks, with-out seats or any shelter from the weather; they were called "stand-up carriages." Those people who had to travel what was then considered a long distance, and wished for some degree of comfort, brought camp stools to sit on, or even brought empty boxes, and converted them into seats.

The old Prison, with its warning inscription of "Whoso keepeth the law is wise," is still standing; when the stocks were removed from the Cross, they were put in front of this building. By the Prison was the "pinfold" or pound, in which stray horses and cattle were placed until claimed by their owners. There was at one time, I have been told, a "ducking-stool" by the river, but that I never saw; its use was to cool the tempers of scolding women, who were fastened on it, and dipped in the water until they learnt how to keep their tongues still-for that time at least.

This has passed away in common with many other old customs of Elland, and much of its ancient beauty. Only under one aspect can it be considered to have gained something in this respect: when, thinning woods, disfigured hills, and un-picturesque buildings, being hidden by the veil of darkness, the streets are outlined by glittering rows of lamps, long lines of lights stretch up the valleys, the hillsides sparkle here and there with lights like fallen stars, and the mills, so uncompromisingly hideous by daylight, blaze from roof to basement as if they were enchanted palaces,---then we may in some measure forget the changes seen in daylight hours, and say that Elland is still beautiful.

Whose
Keepeth the Law is Wise
1821

THE OLD
PRISON
and STOCKS
at ELLAND

This page is Intentionally left blank

OLD CUSTOMS

THERE were many customs connected with the various seasons, not perhaps peculiar to Elland, but yet of interest, because many of them are now dying out.

Getting ready for Christmas used to be a serious business; plum puddings, mince pies, and Christmas cake, were made in large quantities. We always had three kinds of cake: a very rich one, for use on special occasions; one not quite so rich, for ordinary use; and a plain kind of cake or "spice bread," which was eaten with cheese; this " spice bread," together with cheese and beer, were ready in most houses for kitchen company at Christmas time.

In the very early hours of Christmas morning, we were awakened by the choir singing "Christians, awake," with the last line of each verse repeated by way of emphasis; , they were followed by the singers from the various chapels, and all came later in the day for a " Christmas box." The little children also came round singing Christmas hymns, and on New ,Year's Eve they came to sing the "Wessel Song":

HERE we come a wesseling,
Among the leaves so green,
Here we come a wandering,
So fair to be seen.

Cho.---Love and joy come to you,
And to your wessel too,
And God send you a happy year,
A new year,
And God send you a happy new year.

Our wessel cup is made of the rosemary tree,
So is your beer of the best barley,
We are not daily beggars,
That beg from door to door,

But we are neighbours' children,
Whom you have seen before.

91 Old Customs

Call up the butler of this house,
Put on his golden ring,
Let him bring us up a glass of beer
And the better we shall sing.

We have got a little purse,
Made of stretching leather skin,
We want a little of your money,
To line it well within.

Bring us out a table,
And spread it with a cloth,
Bring us out a mouldy cheese,
Likewise a Christmas loaf.

God bless the master of this house,
Likewise the mistress too,
And all the little children,
That round the table go.

Good master and mistress,
While you're sitting by the fire,
Pray think of us poor children,
Who are wandering in the mire.

On that last evening of the year. unless we
kept our doors locked, our houses were
invaded by troops of "mummers," who,
dressed in various odd costumes, and armed
with brushes, came to "sweep the old year
out."

The custom of sending Valentines was very general at one time, but they could only be obtained at the Post Office, and consisted mainly of hideous caricatures; the wonderful contrivances of lace paper, pictures, silk, and scent, were a creation of later years, and the old custom has been almost superseded by the more modern one of sending Christmas cards.

On "April Fools' Day" any tricks were allowable, and curious ones were sometimes played ; for example, I remember that once my cousin sent for Stansfield the tailor on that day, as though my father wished to give him an order, and when the servant at our house found out that he had played such a trick on the poor tailor, she in turn sent my cousin to wait for my father on the bridge so that he might carry a message for him, and it was only after waiting in vain for an hour that he realised that he too had been made an " April fool."

On Good Friday there were dinners of salt
fish in many houses; salt cod, a usual dish,
was indeed fast-day fare; salt herring
somewhat more tolerable; and most people
baked " Friday cakes" or hot cross buns.

Elland Fair was held chiefly at the Cross,
Where I suppose the market was held long
ago. I think I am correct in saying that in old
days every new Sovereign was proclaimed
at Elland before Halifax, in virtue of the
charter for a market granted in the reign of
Edward II. But Elland lost its market; some
say in the time of the plague, when nearly all
the people died, and grass grew in the
streets, some say by sheer laziness and lack
of enterprise. Elland Fair, in my early days;
consisted of a number of shows and booths
containing what to our eyes seemed very
wonderful things; the booths were mostly at
the Cross, and the dining-room shutters at
the

Parsonage had to be closed to allow the long stall, called "the Bazaar," to stand there; and there were others down Dog Lane, while the shows stood in an adjoining field.

Great preparations used to be made for Gunpowder Plot day by the collecting of wood for bonfires, and much baking of parkin, though what the connection is between treacle and meal and gunpowder, or whether, as has been suggested, Guy Fawkes had rather a weakness for parkin I have never found anyone able to say with certainty, but great quantities Were always made and consumed at the beginning of November; and on the night of the historic fifth, the streets were scarcely safe for a peaceable passenger, as crackers and squibs were exploding in all directions.

The old costume of the mill-hands was a pretty and a sensible one; a cotton gown. generally blue, with white spots, and made with short sleeves; a checked apron, a small handkerchief on the head, tidy, well-oiled hair. grey stockings. and the brightest of clogs, and often a coral necklace.

There were no carriages to be hired here in those old days; people going out to tea (they used to go at 5 pm. and leave at 9 p.m.), packed themselves up in readiness for any weather regardless of appearances, and trudged off cheerfully to Greetland or Stainland, or even greater distances. The elder ladies all were caps, and they used to put on "calashes," which were made of silk and whalebone, and were in shape like the hood of a perambulator, so that they could be pushed back or pulled forward for shelter as occasion demanded With these over their caps, and muffled in shawls, the elderly ladies defiled the elements, though waterproof cloaks had not been invented, and umbrellas were still uncommon. What did all these people do without umbrellas? And yet, when they came they were scarcely appreciated, for I have often heard my mother say that my uncle, who lived at Marshall Hall, was the first man in Elland to carry an umbrella, and his father offered him half-a-guinea not to carry it to Church.

While we view umbrellas now with perfect composure, we should think it very strange to see anyone going to Church in pattens, and yet this was commonly done in days gone by; indeed, it is only elderly people who now remember them at all : they consisted of a wooden sole with straps across the foot to keep it on, and a ring of iron under the middle of the sole which raised the patten and its wearer safely out of the muddy roads-and they were muddy then!

THE GREAT SYCOMORE TREE

This page is Intentionally left blank

A gentleman's evening dress was somewhat different then from the style in the present day; when my father went out to dinner he wore a tail coat, black silk stockings, "smalls" and knee buckles. At dinners, the fashion was for all the dishes to be placed on the table at once, which often meant a dozen or more. The custom of "taking wine" was much observed. A gentleman would say to a lady "May I have the pleasure of taking wine with you?". then wine was poured into their glasses, and they drank, first bowing politely to each other. Gentle-men also took wine together.

It would have been considered very strange to see a gentleman walking by the side of a lady without offering her his arm ; my father always made me take his arm when I walked with him.

"Afternoon tea" was then unheard

of, but cake and wine were always brought out for all visitors.

It was considered right that a child's first journey should be to God's House to receive the blessing of Holy Baptism, nor would our mothers visit anywhere until they had returned thanks, or been "churched."

When a child had been baptised, it often received certain peculiar gifts at the first house it visited; these were money, an egg, bread, salt, and a match. This was always the custom at our house, and I believe also at the Parsonage, and at many others. I suppose there is some symbolical meaning in this custom,--my mother explained it thus :- money, to signify wealth; bread, the staff of life; and salt, the seasoning; the child was to be as full of good works as an egg is of meat; and the match was to light the understanding.

When people came to be married, they were said to "stand before Moses and Aaron," in allusion to the pictures at the east end of the Church. We used to watch them from the old Parsonage, and some were very gay with their white horses and scarlet postillions. But hired carriages were not to be had here, so those who possessed none had to walk or come on horseback. Many people now living can tell of their parents doing this; I have heard of some who came walking from Norland with a fiddler in front of them on horseback, playing a merry tune to help them on their journey; and there was once a wonderful wedding party which came from Blackley riding on donkeys, and having for headgear hats made out of Blackley earthenware. In old days all marriages had to be solemnized in Church, but when Queen Victoria came to the throne marriages before a registrar became legal, and at first the editor of the Halifax Guardian used to show that there is a difference between such marriages and those which take place in Church, by putting them last and by heading the list with the words "United by Act of Parliament."

The first time I remember seeing a box of matches was in 1839; they cost fourpence a box; before this, light was obtained by a tinder box, at which matches were lighted having brimstone at each end; these were brought to the door and sold for a half-penny a bundle. Sugar was then ninepence per pound, tea five or six shillings, flour three and Sixpence to five shillings the stone. A neck of mutton was fourpence a pound, fowls from one shilling to one-and-sixpence each, eggs twenty-four for a shilling, brought in from the country in a handkerchief, or a basket

with a little hay at the bottom. Blackberries
were twopence a quart; they abounded in the
woods around, and it was a favourite holiday
with the children to " go a blaggin."

Letters were expensive luxuries; when we
were at school a letter cost ten pence to
send, and we had to pay twopence on
receiving it. Franks were in use up to the
time of the penny post, and were much
sought after; at first a franked letter was one
from a Member of Parliament, who had
signed his name upon it. In the early days of
the Post Office, the privilege which a
Member of Parliament could claim of
sending letters or parcels without payment
was often much abused, and some very
queer things were sent, such as "a deal case
with four flitches of bacon " ; " fifteen
couple of hounds"; " two maid-servants,
going as laundresses to my Lord

Ambassador Methuen." Even after the privilege of free transmission was strictly confined to letters, it was still much abused, for Members of Parliament used to sign large numbers of covers at once and supply their friends with them ; sometimes they were sold, or given to servants in lieu of wages; when I remember, all franks had to be dated, and all such franked letters had to be posted on that date.

I have said that Bazaars were not inevitable things in the old days, but we had them occasionally. I well remember a very pretty little Bazaar we had when at school in Southport; it was very picturesque, being held in the garden, with the articles for sale placed on little tables scattered about. Two little girls stood at the door, prettily dressed in white muslin, with blue sashes and braces; they held baskets to receive the entrance money.

This was our first taste of Bazaars; the proceeds were for the Provident Society, but so much was realised that it was divided between two other societies. We used to make wax tapers for Bazaars, by getting white cotton cord, which we untwisted and dipped in melted wax of various colours; these tapers were sold for Sixpence a bundle of twenty-five.

Elland had then no policemen; the constable was the guardian of the peace, but late at night there was a great deal of fighting and swearing, and many drunken rows.

Gas, of course, was unknown ; and on the nights when that "parish lantern" the moon did not shine, streets and roads were dark indeed. If we had to go out on moonless nights, we carried lanterns to show us the way. One consequence of the darkness was, that stories of spectres or "boggarts" abounded, and no doubt many practical jokes were played. One well-known apparition bore the name of "Long Wall Mouse," so called, I understand, not on account of its size, but of its quietness. Dr. Hiley once told me that ' he had seen this, and it made his hair stand on end: it was a ghostly white mouse which visited " Long Wall " after dark; it was said that whoever saw it was sure to meet with some misfortune, and people were so' afraid of it that the place was always avoided after nightfall.

A most circumstantial story belonged to what was called "Leatherty Coit." It was said that a traveller was once foully murdered in the old "Fleece Inn," and that bloodstains still remained where the dreadful deed was done; stains which no amount of scrubbing or soft soap could ever obliterate, and that those who dared to

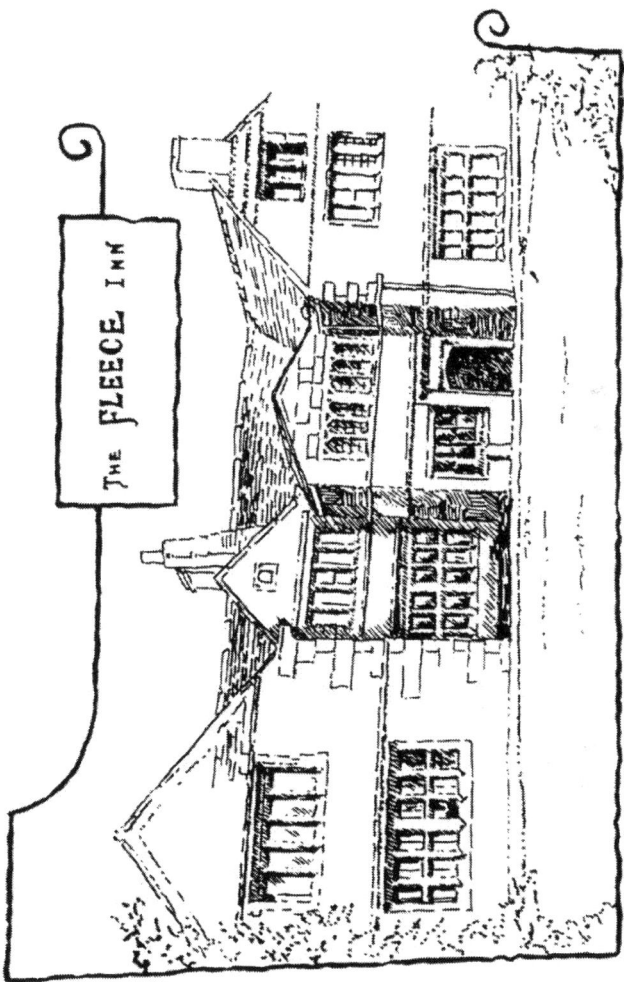

The FLEECE Inn

This page is Intentionally left blank

watch might see an awful sight, for at midnight-I am not sure whether this happened every night, or only at certain seasons the doors of a large barn at the top of Westgate slowly opened without human agency, and there issued forth a travelling carriage with headless horses and headless coachman, Who drove furiously down Dog Lane to Old Earth, and thence returned.

The coming of the spectral vision appears to have been usually accompanied by a sudden rush of wind, however quiet the night, and one can imagine how a sleeper, wakened suddenly by a violent gust or an unexpected noise, would listen trembling, and say, " there goes Leatherty Coit!"

One night in the month of January. a man and his wife were returning home about midnight from the house of a sick relative, and just as they reached the spot where the Railway Hotel now stands there came the gust of wind, and "Leatherty Coit" and his dreadful horses dashed by while they clung to each other in terror.

Another strange thing I heard of long ago: my father's two little brothers were playing out of doors at their home in Northowram, when they suddenly ran into the house in great excitement, saying they had seen such a strange sight- a carriage with two horses had gone by, and the horses and the driver had no heads! They were not afraid, but much surprised.

THE CLERGY OF ELLAND

THE first incumbent of Elland in my remembrance was the Rev. C. Atkinson; he always spent the mornings in his study, and his afternoons in visiting. As I have said elsewhere, he was a High Churchman of those days: he was incumbent for forty years.

His son, the Rev. William Atkinson, was his successor, and held the living for seven years, when he died after a very short illness. He had prepared some candidates for Confirmation, but, being unable through his sudden illness to take them to Halifax, sent a message to my Sister and myself asking us to go with them, which we accordingly did, walking both ways. He used to hold services in the conservatory at Fixby, there being at that time no Mission Room at the Lower Edge; the West window was given to the Church in memory of Mr William Atkinson and his father, and a new lectern and reading desk were bought with the residue of the money. Had Mr. William Atkinson lived longer he would have restored the Church, for that was his desire and intention.

This was also the intention of the next incumbent, the Rev. D. Meredith, but he also died before carrying out his plans. He had the Church lighted with gas, and commenced evening services; during his incumbency the old Parsonage House was sold, and the building of a new one begun, and in the meantime he lived at Calder Cottage; it was in memory of him that the present pulpit was erected.

The Rev. E. Sandford came to Elland in May, 1853, and lived at Calder Cottage until November, when he removed to the new Parsonage. In 1868 he availed himself of "The District Church Tithes' Act, 1865," and purchased Battye's Tithes, and by annexing them permanently to the living gained for himself and his successors the title of Rector of Elland, and the new Parsonage became the Rectory. While Mr. Sandford was here the Church was restored, and a new organ was built. He used to have an annual Christmas Tree for some Church purpose. In his time also the Pitchforth, Hirst, and Rawson windows were given, the cemetery was made, and Greetland Church was built.

Mr. Sandford left for Denford in 1872, and was succeeded by the Rev. F. Musosn. whose memory still lives in the hearts of many of the people of Elland. In his time the present organ was built, the money being raised entirely by voluntary subscriptions. and there being more money than was needed, what remained was used for the purchase of a new lectern; later on the reading desk was replaced by stalls.

While Mr. Musson was with us, the Church had many gifts, including the Hiley, Thwaite, Wilkinson, and Holdsworth windows; he died in 1893, and was succeeded by our present Rector, the Rev. E. Winter.

It is scarcely necessary to speak of the much good work done in the last eight years, but we may mention that the security of the Church tower has been assured; the churchyard levelled, planted. and lighted; and additions and improvements made to the National Schools, both at Elland and Elland Edge, the cost of

ALL SAINTS
ELLAND

This page is Intentionally left blank

the alterations at the Schools alone
amounting to £3,500, and I trust that
sufficient means will be forthcoming to
enable us soon to crown the list by the
completion of the new Church of All Saints.
which is to provide for the rapidly growing
population on the south-west of the town.

There were assistant curates of Elland in the
eighteenth century, but the first assistant
curate of Elland whom I remember was the
Rev. Alex. Charles Fraser, who could speak
seven languages. When a baby he had the
honour of being held in the arms of
Napoleon I. He had, while in Elland,
apartments in the house of a Miss Milnes,
who was a dwarf, and one evening after
service, going in rather unexpectedly, he
found her on a. chair in front of the mirror
decked in his robes. This she told me
herself; also the

reproof she got for her action. After Mr.
Fraser left Elland, he was chaplain to Lord
Clarence Paget, on his vessel L'Aigle, and
while cruising, in the Mediterranean
preached in modern Greek. After him came
the Rev. Hugh Stamer, and he was followed
by the Rev. Geo. Walter Robinson, whose
memory still survives in a volume of
sermons that he published.

The Rev. Charles Heath came next; he
married my mother's youngest stepsister,
and went from here to Birmingham; and
after Mr. Heath came the Rev. George
Langton Beckwith ; he lived with his mother
and sisters at Calder Cottage; they were a
charming family. Then came the Rev.
Francis Innes Jones, and he lived with his
sister at Ivy Cottage. Miss Jones afterwards
went to New Zealand, and travelled among
the aboriginal tribes who had a very short
time before been cannibals.

During these journeys she was once left alone with natives for one or two days, including Sunday, and by the aid of an interpreter, read to them S. John xiv., and then they began to ask her questions. They asked her whether the Queen's palace in England was like the many mansions of which she had been reading. She said the heavenly mansions were much more beautiful; they then asked whether the Queen's palace was guarded by living lions, and she answered: No! the Queen had no more to fear from her subjects than she herself had to fear from them. The chief then offered her a large fat caterpillar, which she declined, saying it was not white man's food, whereupon he gobbled it up himself very quickly. When she left them, they honoured her by presenting her with a spear, the possession of which had been a disputed point among the tribes.

Mr. Jones was succeeded by the Rev. F. Musson, who I am told was the first to begin services at Elland Edge, and took a great interest in that place. Two later curates were the Rev. J. R. Coghlan and the Rev. Robert Rutherford, both of whom preached very well; and the latter always learnt his sermons off by heart. While Mr. Rutherford was here there was a Whitsuntide school feast at How Royd, the very little ones going in waggons, the elder ones walking. I remember this because When they came in sight of the water in Mr. Outram's dam they thought it so pretty that they all clapped their hands in delight. '

The genial personality of the Rev. R. G. Irving is still known in the neighbourhood. When curate here he took a special interest in the young men, and had a large Sunday class of them; when Mr.

Irving left, his place was taken by the Rev.
A. Barrington Orr, who was exceedingly
musical, and kind-hearted; to give pleasure
to the people he often left his windows open
while he performed on the piano; he was
fond of giving tea parties when his sister
was staying with him, to the Sunday school
teachers ; and it is said that on the Fifth of
November, when squibs and crackers were
exploding everywhere according to custom,
he sat at his open window and joined in the
sport by throwing out fireworks, protecting
himself, however, with an umbrella-but I did
not see this.

The Rev. W. J. Kendle came as curate to Mr
Sandford, and remained for some years after
Mr. Musson came as Rector. He worked
very well at Elland Edge, beginning a
reading-room there, which flourished for
some time after he left; he married my
brother Ernest's daughter in

1881, and went to Forston, in Dorsetshire, where he was chaplain to the County Asylum.

Later curates belong to modern history and they must Wait for a more modern historian to record their achievements ; but these are their names and dates:

	1881 Frederick Vaughan.
Rector;	1884 Jonathan George.
Rev.	1886 W. A. Pickering.
F.	1888 Charles Primrose.
Musson.	1890 John Seller.
	1891 David Scott.

	1893-5 Arthur J. B. Ellerton.
	1895 Joseph Holdom.
Rector:	1895-7 H. R. Norris.
Rev.	1895-00 A. B. R. Body.
E.	1897-01 Latimer Fuller.
Winter.	1900 N. Ll. Jenkins.
	1900 G. W. Borlase.

SOME PEOPLE OF ELLAND.

In seventy and odd years a great number of actors pass across the stage of even a little town, and many of those whom I have known have grown too indistinct in my memory for definite reminiscences, but I have gathered together into this last chapter some of those who were best known.

Mr. Hiley, whom I have mentioned as being the only doctor in Elland when my father came to the town, was succeeded in his practice by his second son;. his eldest son was educated as a physician, but he afterwards took Holy Orders; he married a Miss Watkinson for his first wife, and after her death married

a Mrs. Twining and lived at Woodhouse, in
Leicestershire. Old Mr. Hiley had three sons
and three daughters ; they were a most
generous family.

Miss Hiley used to help us when we
collected money in those days for Church
purposes; I remember going once with her
for this purpose to Shaw Laithe, where Mr.
A. Pitchforth lived, and when he was not
very ready in giving us anything I
laughingly suggested that if he did not help
us we should have to go to prison;
whereupon he replied: " Ah, you would be
very nice company for them"; but he gave us
a subscription. This Mr. Pitchforth married a
sister of Mr. John Wilkinson who lived at
Beech Grove; and he married Miss Terry
Atkinson, sister of the Vicar, ' Mr. William
Atkinson, and was always a great helper to
the Church.

At this time the Ashworths lived at

Staircase
at
Marshall Hall

This page is Intentionally left blank

Bank House; the old Baptist chapel in
Jepson Lane belonged to them, and in 1894
the Miss Ashworths gave the building to the
Rector and Churchwardens of Elland to be
used for Church purposes, and at the same
time endowed it with a fund for putting it
and keeping it in repair.

An uncle of ours, Mr. Benjamin Rushforth,
lived at Marshall Hall; one of our
illustrations shows the staircase of that
house, and of it I have very happy
recollections: when my great uncle had
some of his grandchildren staying with him,
my sister and I used to go and play with
them; at the foot of the stairs where they
meet the flight leading to the opposite
gallery there used to stand a large statue, and
our favourite game was to play at being in
Church; one of the boys would sit on the
statue and another at its foot, as parson and
clerk, and we sat on the stairs and formed
the congregation.

At the house now called Westgate House used to live old Mr. Jonathan Crowther, and in the days of his son, Mr. Charles Crowther, we children used to go to his garden to eat delicious fruit; this we liked very much, but especially on account of certain splendid red currants which grew there.

A very sad thing is connected in my mind with this family; one of the daughters married my uncle Northend, and three weeks after his marriage he was killed ; they were living at Castle Hill,.Rastrick, and he had gone to shoot at Fixby Park, when suddenly the keeper heard the report of his gun and saw him fall; he was carried into the house but died in a few hours; it was supposed that in getting over a hedge he had caught the trigger of his gun in a branch, but the keeper was not near enough to know certainly; it was a very great shock to my father, and from that day he never could bear even the name of Fixby.

Some years after the Crowthers had left Elland, Westgate House was taken by Mr. Joseph Wilson and did not lose its importance for Elland, as his eldest son, Mr. John Wilson, became the first resident magistrate that Elland ever possessed.

Among official persons I must name Amos Crowther, a well-known and much valued Elland man ; he and his father were sextons successively at S. Mary's for many years; he was very musical, the instrument he excelled in being the Violoncello; and at all oratorios and at most of the concerts in the neighbourhood he was one of the performers; he was married, and one of his daughters, Naomi, married Mr. Wm. Robison. In those days we had the "Messiah" and selections from the

"Creation," in the school every Christmas,

when we gathered together all the musical talent of the neighbourhood, amongst the performers being our celebrated Yorkshire soprano, Mrs. Sunderland, Who delighted everyone With her singing of "I know that my Redeemer liveth," and " With Verdure clad." '

Another person well-known in Elland, though not living there, was Mr. Richard Oastler, sometimes called "The Factory King." He was stewed for Mr Thornhill, and lived at Fixby Hall, from whence he used to come to Elland Church on foot, his wife With him, riding on a donkey.

He worked hard for the passing of the Ten Hours' Bill, and so gained the affections of the factory workers that some old people can still remember snatches of a song composed and sung in his honour. the chorus being something like this :-

Three cheers, three cheers for Oastler,
While we our breath can gain,
Because he stands up for the poor,
Their rights for to maintain.

Unfortunately, he seems to have been a
better philanthropist than business man, for
he got wrong in his accounts, and was sent
to the Fleet Prison; on his release there was
great enthusiasm, and crowds of people
flocked to Brighouse to welcome him. A
statue was erected to his memory in
Bradford, which represents him with two
little factory children clinging to him ; and
in the graveyard of Christ Church,
Woodhouse, near Huddersfield, a monument
speaks of him thus :

"The memory of Richard Oastler lives in the
hearts of thousands. He was a true patriot;
loyal to his Sovereign ; faithful to the
Church of his country; the oppressed, the
friendless, and the poor, (above all, the
hapless factory workers,) found in him an
able and fearless advocate."

Among the Elland people of my young days
there were two old gardeners of the name of
Wood-Joseph and Abraham. who, with
Sammy Balmforth, were examples in being
always at Holy Communion ; and another
regular Church-goer was Abraham Marsden,
who never missed a Church service for forty
years. At one election, when, I think,
Morpeth and Milton were the candidates,
my father tried to instil 'into the old Woods
which candidate to vote for. The system of
voting by ballot had not then been
introduced; all had to vote by word of
mouth, and went to Halifax for that pur-m
pose. Alas! when Joseph and Abraham
arrived there, all their careful teaching was
forgotten, and their votes were lost, for, on
being asked for whom they voted, one said
"Church and King," the other " Same as
Doctor Hamerton." Abraham went about
with a large blue or green cotton

umbrella, after the manner of Mrs. Gamp.
He was very charitable, but so afraid of
being thanked that he gave his gifts in a
peculiar way; he would stand with his
back to the table and his hands behind him
until he had deposited his gifts there, and
then would get out of the house as quickly
as possible.

" Water Molly," so called because she
carried water for any who were willing to
pay for having it brought, instead of carrying
it for themselves, was another regular
Church-goer and communicant; she was also
a great lover of cats, of which she had a
large number. She met with a sad end; one
Good Friday she went to Church as usual; it
was a very wet day, so on reaching home
she sat down near the tire to dry her clothes-
too near! for her clothes caught fire, and
poor Molly was burnt to death.

"Fish Molly" was another old Elland character; she provided the fish for Elland, and was very deaf. She used an eartrumpet, and could hear through it very well when you ordered some fish, but if the answer was "None to-day, Molly," she immediately became very deaf indeed, and the ear-trumpet of no use at all!

The verger of our early days was rather a terrific person; naughty children were often frightened into obedience by the threat of being given to "Old Cabbage." When, as little children, we went alone to Church, we had to conquer our fear of this imposing being in scarlet plush, and ask him to open the door of our pew, as it was a very high one, with a bolt inside, unapproachable by short arms and tiny lingers.

Our late verger, James Luty, was for many years one of the chief features of

Elland. He was quite an original character, and curious tales could be told of his sayings and doings. On one occasion, when a number of clergy were at the Church, he went to the vestry and said that the Bishop of Copley wished to Speak to the Bishop of Hebden Bridge.

Another time,--this was on Whit-Sunday, 1893-at a late Celebration of Holy Communion, on taking up the offertory to the altar and telling the Rector how many were present, he said out aloud, "Theer's twenty-eight, but two as hasn't paid." He was very strong and active as a young man, and used to tell how, in those days, he could run to the top of the Ainleys without stopping, but in his later days he grew very feeble, and suffered much from rheumatism and young curates; he died in the autumn of 1900.

PART II

BY

J. w. CLAY, F.S.A.

The Early history of Elland

IT almost seems a pity that the ancient and more elegant name, of Ealand or Eland has been altered in modern times to that of Elland. Its derivation appears to be from the Anglo-Saxon 'Ea-land, land on the side of a river.

There is not much to be said about the early history 'of this place. At one time it was thought that its neighbour, Greetland, might have been the site of the Roman town of Cambodunum, but that theory is now exploded, although perhaps there might have been a small station there, as a Roman altar is said to have been found in the time of Queen Elizabeth.

Elland is mentioned in Doomsday book as forming, with Southowram, part of the lands of Ilbert de Laci, the great lord of Pontefract, and it has always since remained in the Honor of Pontefract, Whilst Halifax and the rest of the parish have belonged to the Warrens and to the Manor of Wakefield.

From the Lacies it came, we do not exactly know how, to the family of Eland, who, for several generations, were the lords. No doubt most persons have read the ballad of Sir John Eland of Eland and his antagonists, commonly called "the Elland Feud." The story put into prose is this:- Sir John Eland, on account of some quarrel, gathered together his friends and tenants, and one night went to Quarmby Hall.

To Quarmby Hall they came by night,
And there the lord they slew,
At that time Hugh of Quarmby hight,
Before the country knew.

The same night they slew Lockwood of Lockwood, and then went on to Crosland Hall and killed Sir Robert Beaumont of that place.

The lady cried and shrieked withal,
When as from her they led
Her dearest Knight into the hall,
And there cut off his head. .

The Lady Beaumont fled with her two sons into Lancashire, and there remained for some years. When they had grown up they returned, and, assisted by Lacy and Lockwood and two men from Quarmby, Dawson and Haigh, lay in wait for Sir John Eland in Cromwell-bottom Woods, on his way from keeping the turn at Brighouse.

They cut him from his company,
Belike at the Lane end ;
And there they slew him certainly,
And thus he made his end.

After this Adam Beaumont and his fellows tied to Furness fells, where they remained for some time waiting for further revenge. Then one Palm Sunday evening they broke into Elland Mill and waited for young Sir John Eland, son of the Sir John whom they had previously slain: As the young Knight was crossing the dam stones to go to Church, with his armour on, he was attacked by Beaumont and Lockwood, and shot through the head and killed. His young son was also wounded, and finally died in Elland Hall. The inhabitants of Elland rose up and pursued the murderers.

Quarmby was slain in Ainley Wood, but Adam Beaumont managed to escape and fled to Crosland Hall. The ballad does not say what became of him.

Such is a short account of this bloody fray, and although the ballad has been printed by Watson and other Halifax historians, its truth has been much doubted; Mr. Paley Baildon. F.S.A., has however

recently found some evidence at the Record
Office, in London, which seems to confirm
it. In 1353, Robert del Both, of Holmfirth,
and three other men, were had up at York
Castle before the Justice of the King, for
having received William Lockwood of
Lockwood and Adam Beaumont when they
had feloniously killed Sir john de Bland, and
Thomas Molot was also charged with having
received Thomas Lacey. Again in 1355,
John de Shelley was had up at York for
having received William Lockwood, Adam
Beaumont, and others who had killed Sir
John Eland; he was found "not guilty."

Sir John Eland was High Sheriff of
Yorkshire in 1341, and is said to have died
in 1350, and this is probable, as his goods
were administered in that year by Dame
Alice, his wife, on the feast of the Nativity
of our Lady. There is one thing in the

Ballad that hardly seems to be correct. After
mentioning the death of the young boy who
had been wounded , it says:-

A full sister forsooth had he,
An half-brother also;
The full sister his heir must be,
The half-brother not so.

The full sister his heir she was,
And Savile wed the same ;
Thus lord of Eland Savile Was,
And since in Savile name.

There is no doubt that Sir John Savile
obtained the Elland property by marrying
Isabella, the heiress of the Elands, but When
he founded the chantry at the Church, the
deed clearly mentions Thomas de Eland, and
Joan his wife, parents of Isabella. It
therefore appears likely that the boy Who
was killed had a younger brother Thomas,
and that the heiress was his daughter, and
grand-daughter of Sir John Eland who was
killed in crossing

The Arms of Savile,
quartering Golcar, Eland, Thornhill

This page is Intentionally left blank

the river. The dates are however rather against this supposition, so it is possible Thomas might be brother, not son of Sir John. The Saviles having thus come into possession have continued to hold a large portion of the land of Elland to the present day.

It is stated that in the reign of Edward I. a charter was granted to Sir John Eland to hold a market and two fairs. When the poll tax was levied in 1379, Elland was assessed at 45s.4d., whilst Halifax had only 12s.8d. to pay, although its position was not as good; Halifax afterwards took the lead and became a more important place, so that the above

market ultimately fell into disuse.

The wars of the Roses do not seem to have interfered with' Elland, and 'we hear nothing of it in those troublous times. The inhabitants probably preferred trade to fighting, as they had settled down to cloth making at a very early period. Even as far back as 1379, in the above poll tax returns there were two merchants and three websters mentioned.

It was probably on account of the profits the Clothiers had made, that towards the beginning of the 16th century Elland was in a very flourishing condition. No doubt many of the halls were then begun to be erected or to be renovated in a better style. Their owners a little later commenced to send their sons to the universities, Sir John Savile going in 1561, and his two brothers soon after, whilst at a later date Robert Clay, and the two Ramsdens who became Vicars of Halifax, the Wilkinsons, 3 Hanson, with others, followed this fashion.

At the Coronation of King Charles I. the chief inhabitants of each place through-

out the country were ordered to be knighted.
To escape this honour many however
refused it, preferring rather to pay a fine. In
Elland-cum-Greetland, Jasper Blythman,
armiger, was fined £25, Anthony Foxcroft,
gentleman, ,£ 15, whilst John Clay, Robert
Inman, Robert Whittell, and John Ramsden,
of High Trees, got off with payinig £10. In
Barkisland, William Horton's fine was £20,
and John Ramsden's £12.

When the Civil War broke out no doubt the
greater part of the inhabitants of this part of
the West Riding were Parliamentarians. The
largest owner in Elland, the non-resident Sir
William Savile, of Thornhill, was a
Commander on the Royal side. Having been
unsuccessful in his attack on Bradford, he
became governor of Sheffield and of York.
where he died in 1644. How it was that his
estates escaped sequestration and sale, and

were differently treated to those of other great royalists is strange, but there seems no mention of any fines in the royalist composition papers in London. Sir John Savile, of Lupset, a near relative, the head of a younger Savile branch, which ultimately succeeded to the estates, took the opposite side and garrisoned Howley Hall for the Parliament. He was an active magistrate, and in the Elland registers it is found, in 1655, that William Baker and

Mary Roundsley were married before Sir John Savile, justice.

The Gledhills of Barkisland were also Royalists; Richard Gledhill was a Captain of Horse under Sir Marmaduke Langdale, and was knighted by the Marquis of Newcastle. He was slain at Hessay-moor in 1644. His brother John had to pay a fine of £127,

Such is a slight sketch of the History

of Elland to the middle of the 17th century.
Since then, although it may have increased
in population and in material prosperity, it
has lost much of its interest for an
antiquarian mind. Many of the old houses,
as New Hall, Elland Hall, and Bradley, have
been turned into farm houses, whilst others
being overshadowed by mills, have lost their
attractiveness.

This page is Intentionally left blank

ELLAND CHURCH

THERE are various opinions whether the Church of Halifax or that of Elland is the older, and it seems doubtful if the question will ever be decided. At any rate there was a Church at Elland at a very early period, but whether as far back as the Norman times it is difficult to say. Some authorities state that the chancel arch may go back nearly to the year 1200, but the greater part of the building probably dates from the fifteenth century.

If the story of the Elland Feud just related is correct, about 1350 Sir John Eland was on his way to Church when he was killed. In 1396 Sir John Savile founded a chantry in the Chapel of Eland to pray for himself and Isabella his wife and their children, his parents John Sayvill and Margaret his wife, and for Thomas de Eland and Joan his wife, parents of the said Isabella. In 1488 Thomas Savile, of Hullen Edge, leaves his wife a messuage, she finding one serge of wax before the image of the Blessed Virgin Mary at Eland Kirke each year. In 1506, Miles Woodhead leaves to the Chapel of Eland for the buying of a bell forty shillings; and no doubt if all the Elland Wills were examined there would be found many benefactions of a like manner to the Church.

The parish of Halifax seems to have been divided ecclesiastically into three parts. The inhabitants of one went to Halifax Church, of another to Heptonstall Church, whilst the remaining part was reserved for Elland. In early times no doubt all the Christenings, Marriages.

and Burials, of this part were solemnized at the parent Church of Elland, and were duly entered in the registers. Then when Rastrick and Ripponden Churches were built, though Christenings might be performed there, they were still entered at Elland. It was not till later times that there were any burials elsewhere than at Elland. There was no burial ground at Rastrick till after 1798.

In the register book in 1667 there is given a list of the churchwardens and presenters, which is interesting as showing which townships belonged to Elland Church, viz. : -Elland-cum-Greetland, Stainland, Barkisland, Rishworth-cum-Norland, Soyland-cum-Fixby, Rastrick-cum-Brighouse. They each had one churchwarden and one presenter.

The Church of Elland must at one time have been very beautiful, with the Savile

and Thomhill chapels full of monuments,
and with the windows filled with stained
glass resplendent with heraldry. There is an
engraving in Watson's History of Halifax, of
a Savile kneeling along with his wife, on
their coats the three owls, the arms of Savile.
Their children are kneeling behind them. A
similar picture of a Thornhill is also given.
A list of coats of arms and some curious
inscriptions, taken about 1584, are copied as
well in Watson. When the great destruction
of the monuments and glass took place is not
known, but there were still some existing in
1669. At the present time, with the
exception of the East window, all the
fragments of old glass that remain are in two
windows at the West end. It is certainly a
curious fact, that of all the wide-spreading
family of Savile, not a vestige of a memorial
remains in the Church. There are some
Thornhill monuments dating from 1669,

which are interesting, with others of a later date.

The chancel was called St. Mary's Quire; the chapel on the South side St. John's Quire, and belonged to the Saviles; that on the North side St. Nicholas's Quire, and belonged to the Thornhills. In 1607, John Thornhill, Esq., willed: " My body I commit to the earth to be buried in my Quire in the Church of Ealand, where divers of my ancestors have been buried."

THE EAST WINDOW.

The glory of Elland Church is the stained glass window at the East end, which is superior to anything of the kind in the parish of Halifax, or perhaps even in any Church for a long distance round. Unfortunately, however, it has been a great deal restored, and of the 21 compartments 10 are entirely modern, namely the five lower ones, the middle and right-hand one in the next higher row, the second from the right on the third row, the second from the left on the fourth row, and the top one of all, whilst the other n have been more or less restored.

When the Yorkshire Archaeological Society visited the Church in 1876, a paper on the window was read by the late Mr. James Fowler, F.S.A., a great authority on old glass. He deplored the restoration and wished it could have been preserved. in its old state, as not only was it a mistake to mix old with modern work, but also the way in which the compartments had been placed had destroyed its history. He considered the date was late fifteenth century, and that the subject was the life of the Blessed Virgin Mary. Mostly from his paper the following description of the compartments is taken :

Assumpta est Maria in cœlum.

From the East Window of S. Marys Elland.

This page is Intentionally left blank

1. The Annunciation to St. Anne.---There lived at Nazareth a just man named Joachim, of the tribe of Judah and of the race of David, with his wife Anne or Hannah. The holy couple lived together in the practice of every virtue, but one great blessing was wanting to them: they were without children which made them sad. At length one day, when Joachim was watching his flocks, the angel appeared to him, and when he was troubled at the vision said, "Fear not, Joachim, thy prayers are heard, wherefore Anne, thy wife, shall bear a daughter, and thou shalt call her name Mary. And of her shall be born the son of the Most High, through whom shall come salvation in all lands, and this shall be a sign, that when thou comest to the golden gate of Jerusalem, thou shalt meet Anne thy wife, who shall rejoice at thy appearing." The angel, bearing a palm in her hand, visits Anne and gives her a message. Beneath is the inscription :- "O Anna gratiosa matris gratiosae."

2. The meeting of Joachim and Anne at the Golden Gate.--The two are embracing preparatory to returning home, there joyfully to await the divine promise. Beneath

is the restored inscription:- "O Joachim sancta conjux Anne."

3. The Birth of the Blessed Virgin.---St. Anne is represented lying in a bed with a richly coloured and fringed tester, holding in her arms a child with long hair, whilst two persons attend behind, and in front the nurse, holding a napkin in her hand, with at her feet a cradle. Beneath the inscription :---" Ante colles ego parturiebar."

4. The woman anointing our Lord's feet and wiping them with her hair- This is quite modern, and bears the inscription-"Sinite illam at in diem sepulurae meae servet illud."

5. The Presentation of our Lord in the Temple. - Quite modern ; the inscription :--" In habitatione sancta coram ipsi ministrare " (this last should perhaps be ministravi.)

6. Betrothal of Mary and Joseph.---They are kneeling, and a figure in episcopal vestments behind is joining their hands, whilst another in lay costume attends. Beneath, the restored inscription :---" Dispensatio (Desponsatio) tua Dei genetrix virgo. "

7. The Assumption of the Virgin.--She is bare-headed, with long golden hair and hands

folded on her bosom, in blue cloak lined with ermine and red under robe, with her richly diapered golden girdle loose and falling off, nimbed and, in a glory upheld by three angels on each side, is being carried up to heaven. The inscription 9-"Assumpta est Maria in caelum."

8. Christ's entry into Jerusalem.--With the inscription :---"Hosanna benedictus qui venit in nomine Domini. "

9. Christ in Glory.--Modern, having no inscription.

10. The Ascension of our Lord. --The Virgin, richly robed, is kneeling on the ground with the' Apostles, whilst our Lord disappears above; the skirts of His robe alone being visible, surrounded by a glory. Beneath is the inscription :---" Ascendit in caelum."

11. The Resurrection.-Our .Lord, naked with the exception of a purple cloth about His loins and loose red cloak fastened at the neck, holding His right hand in benediction, and an ornamental cross in His left, showing the five sacred wounds, is stepping out of an empty tomb guarded by four sleeping soldiers in plate armour. Beneath is the inscription : --" Surrexit Dominus Vere Alleluia. "

12. The Crucifixion.--Quite modern, with the inscription :--" Consummatum est."

13. The Institution of the Eucharist. -» Quite modern, with the inscription :---"Hoc facite in meam commemorationem. "

14. The Adoration of the Magi-The Virgin, richly vested, is seated with the Holy Child on her knee, standing and holding out his hands to receive a basin of golden money offered by a king kneeling bareheaded, with a crown on the ground by his side. Two other kings, crowned, richly robed, wait behind, and behind the Virgin is a stall with a hurdle fence, containing two oxen,' and with two doves upon the roof. Above all,'-in the sky, is a large star emitting rays downward. Below is this inscription :----" Et adorabunt omnes reges." '

15. The Baptism of our Lord.--Quite modern, on a scroll the inscription :-"Meus dilectus est Filius Hic," and below " Et baptizatus est in jordane."

16. The Descent of the Holy Ghost.--Mary, richly robed, is kneeling with hands conjoined, surrounded by the Apostles, whilst above, the Holy Ghost is seen descending as a

FIGURES formerly in ELLAND CHURCH

ELIZABETH   MARY   JANE   DOROTHY

This page is Intentionally left blank

dove, with cruciform nimbus, emitting rays, alternately straight and wavy, downwards. The inscription is :---"Et repleti sunt! omnes spirituunt sancto."

17. The Agony in the Garden.-Quite modern, inscription :-"Non mea voluntas, sed tua' fiat."

18. The Annunciaton.-This is one of the most interesting and perfect of the series. Mary, on her knees before a faldstool on which is an open book, receives the message of the angel, "Ave Maria gratis plena Dns tecum," whilst the angel kneels before her, holding out his right hand in salutation and a golden sceptre in his left. The attitude of the Virgin expresses humble surprise and hesitation as she replies, "Ecce ancilla Dni." Between the Virgin and the angel blossoms a pot of lily, the emblem of virginity. In the upper corner of the compartment is the Ancient of Days in glory, from whom to the ear of the Virgin proceeds a beam of light in the midst of which the Holy Ghost, in form of a. white dove, is seen. Beneath is the inscription :---" Benedicta in mulieribus."

19. The Visitation.--Two women, richly dressed, and standing face to face. Beneath is the inscription :--" Et salutavit Elizabeth. "

20. The Nativity.---Quite modern, bearing the inscription :--" Puer nobis est natus."

21. The Carrying of the Cross.-Quite modern; the inscription :-" Posuit Dominus in ea inquitatem omnium nostrum."

It will therefore be seen that if this window, as stated above, is intended to be a history of , the Virgin, many of the modern compartments are out of place as containing events in the life of our Lord, in which His mother took no special part, such as 4, 8, 9, I3, 17, 21, and that their position is not altogether in proper order.

The plan under will explain the numbers and their position.

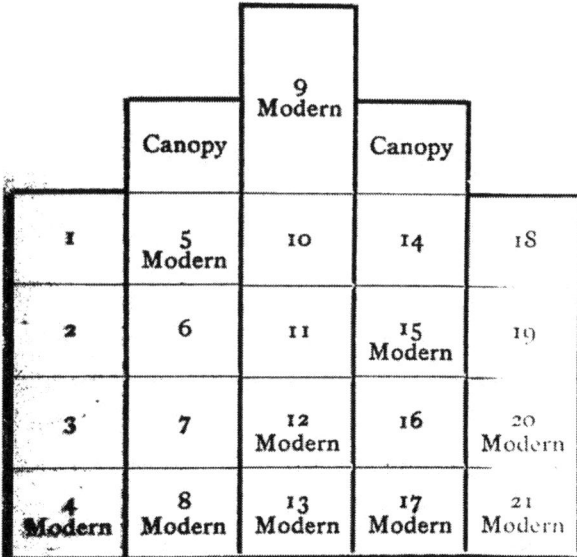

		9 Modern		
	Canopy		Canopy	
1	5 Modern	10	14	18
2	6	11	15 Modern	19
3	7	12 Modern	16	20 Modern
4 Modern	8 Modern	13 Modern	17 Modern	21 Modern

THE REGISTERS.

In 1538 parish registers were ordered to be kept throughout the whole country, and the Halifax ones actually commenced at that date. The Elland registers are 20 years later, the first entry being in April, 1559. They have been printed up to the year 1640, and contain much interesting matter, as there are entries not only from Elland itself but from many neighbouring townships. As previously stated, all the burials were at Elland till modern times, but christenings, if they were performed at the newer Churches, were all entered at the parent Church, although some of the clergy sometimes kept a duplicate register.

In the Elland registers are many entries of the Saviles, the Thornhills of Fixby, the Gledhills and Hortons of Barkisland, the Clays 0f Clayhouse, the Ramsdens and Wilkinsons of Greetland, the Priestleys, Foxcrofts, &c.

CURATES AND INCUMBENTS OF ELLAND.

It seems difficult to make a complete list of the Curates and Incumbents of

Elland, as no doubt in the early days the Curates were under Halifax, and had no distinct cure. Search has been made in the official registers at York, and all the entries there have been taken out, so that the following account, Which includes what is found in the Elland registers, will probably be as correct as it is possible to give.

1459. John Strenger, chaplain of the parochial chapel of Elande.

1544. James Butterfield was curate.
1561. July, Michael Savile, curate of Elande, mentioned.

1565. Dec. 22, Robert Mylner, curate of Elande, buried.

*1566. April, Skolefeld begins. (Not in Watson's list.)

*1577. Dec. 25, Elizabeth, daughter of John Leigh, curate of Elande, baptized. (Mr. Leigh not mentioned by Watson.)

1588. Mar. 24, Richard Worrall, entered into the cure.

*1592. May 1. Adam Wright; clericus, began (Not in Watson.)

1593. April, Costan Mawde, clericus, first entered here, buried 17th Nov., 1600.

*1596. Sept. 25, Joshua Smith entered here. (He is not mentioned by Watson, and it seems strange he should be here before Mr. Mawde died.) '

1601. April, Edward Sunderland, A.M., of Clare Hall, Cambridge. He died 29th Jan, and was buried Ist February, 1632-3. His gravestone is still to be seen in the churchyard. It states he was Master of Artes and Proecher of God's word at Eland almost 32 years, Where he had lived near 74 years. His son Jeremiah, an Oxford scholler who died aged 18, lies near him, along with two other children.

1633. John Thomson, curate. He had a son John baptized in 1636.

1651 and 1653. Robert Houldsworth, mentioned.

1652. ----Abbot.

1652. Robert Towne, mentioned. No date of his coming, but Oliver Heywood says: "At Elland I found, 1650, old Mr. Robert

Towne, the famous Antinomian, who writ some books. He was the best scholar and soberest man of that judgment in the country, but something unsound in principles. He removed: lived and died not long ago a nonconformist."

1656. Mr. R. Walker, minister, mentioned. O. Heywood says: "Then came one Mr. Walker, Who though he professed fair, yet he proved a man-pleasing temporizer at the change of the times. He went into the North; is dead. His widow lives at Gisburn.','

1663. Josiah Broadhead He became vicar of Batley. Instituted there, 25th April, 1667; buried in the Church there, 6th July, 1685.

1667-8. Peter Ashton, AM. He was buried at Elland, Nov. 3, 1698. The inscription on his gravestone in the chancel is given by Watson. It is not now in existence.

1699. Richard Petty, March 5.

1721. Jeremiah Bairstow, died July 28, 1731.

1733. George Smith, died Dec. 4.

160 Olde Eland

1734 Thomas Alderson, M.A., admitted to the curacy June 14, on the nomination of the Vicar of Halifax

1746 William Stackhouse, clerk, admitted the curacy July12.

1761 Robert Ogden, resigned Dec. 19.
Samuel Ogden D.D.

1768 George Burnett, M.A., admitted to the curacy on resignation of Samuel Ogden, D.D., upon the nomination of the Vicar of Halifax.

1793 Thomas -Watson,4'clerk, licensed to the perpetual curacy of Elland, on death of George Burnett, clerk, Dec. 3.

1802 Christopher Atkinson, M.A., licensed to the perpetual curacy of Elland.

1843 William Atkinson.

1849 David Meredith.

1853 Edward Sandford.

1872 Francis Musson.

1893 Ernest Winter.
N.B.---Those marked with an asterisk (*)are not in the York registers.

Elland Hall

BRIDGE COTTAGE

This page is Intentionally left blank

FAMILIES OF ELLAND.

THE ELANDS OF ELLAND HALL.

THIS house, from its appearance at the present time, does not look as if it had ever been a very noble building, but it must have been at one time the most important residence in the parish. For several generations the Elands probably resided there. As stated in the account of the "Elland Feud," Sir John Eland was killed about 1350, and his son soon after. The pedigree states that Thomas Eland succeeded, and by Joan his wife had a daughter and heiress who married Sir John Savile; and so the family. died out at Elland, although a younger branch was settled near Batley, and at Hull.

THE SAVILES OF ELLAND HALL.

This family probably came to Elland from
Golcar. There seems to have been a John
Savile who married Margery Rushworth or
Rishworth. They had a son, Sir John Savile,
who married the heiress of Eland. He
became an important man, being High
Sheriff of Yorkshire in 1380, 1383, and
1388, and Knight of the Shire. We have his
Will in I 399, by which he desires to be
buried at Elland. Before his death he had
founded a. chantry at Elland Church, to pray
for his own, his wife's, his father's and his
mother's souls. He had two sons, the eldest
of Whom, Sir John, succeeded to Elland,
whilst the second son Henry made a great
match with the heiress of the Thornhills of
Thornhill. Their son ultimately succeeded to
both Thornhill and Elland in consequence of
his cousin dying issueless. Elland Hall
seems then to have been deserted as a
residence for

Thornhill, and probably was never permanently occupied afterwards by the Saviles at a later tune the house was Constantly let to various tenants.

Henry Savile, who married the Thornhill heiress, had two sons, of whom the younger Henry married the Copley heiress, and was ancestor of most of the many branches which spread over Elland and its neighbourhood.

The eldest son, Sir Thomas, was a. Knight of the Shire in 1439; from him descended the main line at Thornhill and Elland. ' '

Much influence and emolument came to its members from their being stewards of the great Manor of Wakefield, and sometimes custodians of ' the castle at Sandal. When Sir Henry Savile died in 1558, it was found that he had 22,080

acres of land besides the great wastes
and commons not included.

Sir William Savile was a Commander on the
Royalist side in the civil war. His house at
Thornhill was burnt by the Parliamentarians,
and the family then removed to Rufford
Abbey. His son, of whom so much is written
in Lord Macaulay's history, was created by
Charles II. Baron Eland, Earl and Marquis
of Halifax. There were two Lord Elands who
both died in their father's life-time. The last
of the main line, Sir George Savile, seventh
Baronet, was M.P. for Yorkshire, but dying
in 1743, and having never married, the
Elland and other Yorkshire estates passed to
his sister Barbara, who had married the Earl
of Scarborough. They are ancestors of the
present Lord Savile.

THE SAVILES OF HULLINEDGE.

Henry Savile, who married the Thornhill heiress, had a second son, Who, having married another heiress, the daughter of Thomas Copley, of Copley, founded the Copley Saviles. From his second son Thomas descended several other branches; he himself became of Hullinedge, and dying about 1457, left a son John Who is described as being Squire of the Body to King Edward the Fourth, and as ancestor of four generations at Hullinedge. There is little known of them, and they are only twice mentioned in the Elland registers. The last of the line was buried there 16th March, 1609-10, and his wife Dorothy 22nd August, 1614. They are said to have had two daughters, Isabel and Jane, but what became of them or how he property passed away does not appear.

THE SAVILES OF NEWHALL.

This quaint old house, now, alas, only a
farm house, is seen on the hillside above the
road from Rastrick to Elland. It was built by
and was for a long time the abode of this
branch of the Savile family. Thomas Savile,
of Hullinedge, mentioned in the account of
that place, had a fourth son called Nicholas,
Who, in his turn founded several branches, '
He possessed Newhall, and his eldest son'
John succeeded him and made his will in
1540, 'We have a little more information
about these Saviles as there are many wills
at York, and several entries in the registers.
They also lived at Kexborough. in South
Yorkshire, The last of the line at Newhall,
John Savile, had only four daughters, and
perhaps on that account agreed to sell the
estate in his life-time. He was buried
at Elland, 17th April, 1620, his wife
Frances, a daughter of Godfrey Bosvile,
dying

New Hall, Elland.

This page is Intentionally left blank

him. There are entries in the registers of the burials of two of his daughters, and of the marriage of another named Dorothea to Thomas Gifford, of Essex.

Newhall passed into the hands of the Foxcrofts. In 1656, Dr.. Henry Power, F.R.S., Who had married a daughter of Anthony Foxcroft, was living there. He had a first-rate practice amongst the gentry in the neighbourhood. Several of his account books are amongst the Sloane M.SS. in the British Museum, with copies of his prescriptions and bills which deserve publication.

Dr. Power did not live very long at Newhall ; he went to Wakefield in 1664, where he continued his practice. He died 23rd Dec. 1668, and was buried in Wakefield Church. There is an account of him in the Dictionary of National Biography.

THE SAVILES OF BRADLEY.

From this branch, although it was a younger one, several of the most celebrated members of the Savile family have sprung. For its origin we must return to the New-hall Saviles. John Savile of Newhall, mentioned as dying in 1540, had a second son Henry, who appears to have lived at Bradley, and to. have married a Ramsden. His will was made 10th June, 1566, and he was buried at Elland, 12th October the same year. He had three sons, Sir John Savile, Sir Henry Savile, and Thomas Savile of Oxford, all distinguished for their learning. We will deal with them in succession.

Sir John Savile is stated to have been baptised at Elland Church, 26th March, 1546, too early for an entry in the registers. An interesting Auto-biography of him has been lately printed in the journal of the

Yorkshire Archaeological Society. It
States that he received his early education
at Elland and in the neighbourhood, and that
he went to Brazenose College, Oxford,
in March, 1560-1. This would be when he
was 15 years' old. In two years' time he
took the degree of a Bachelor, and on
account of the plague returned to Bradley,
where he read law. He was admitted to the
Middle Temple in February, 1564-5, and
then began to practise in the Northern circuit
in 1574. The next year he married Jane
Garth of Surrey, by whom he had three
children. He built the new house at Bradley,
which was first inhabited in I 580. His wife
died in 1587 aged 32, and in December the
same year he married the widow of Richard
Tempest, Esq.; they had three Children all
born at Bradley ; his second wife died in
1592-3, and he again married a widow,
Dorothy, late wife of Sir Martin Frobisher
the navigator. Having

been previously appointed a Sergeant-at-Law in July, 1598, he was made a Baron of the Exchequer. It was, however, before this time that he bought Methley and began to build the Hall there. Ralph Thoresby of Leeds, in 1709 visited it, and " was mightily pleased with the sight of Methley Hall, which was built in the memorable year (the Armada) 1588, as appears by that date upon the front under the arms of the family." Sir John Savile's third wife was buried there in January, 1601-2. He was knighted 1603 by King James I ., and again married another widow, Margaret Weston. Having been a judge nearly nine years " this singular patron of preachers of God's word quietly fell asleep in the Lord, to the greatest sorrow and grief of all at Serjeant's Inn, London, and lies buried in the Church of St. Dunstan, in-the-West, near Jane his first wife, on the second day of February, 1606-7."

From Sir John Savile descend the only
Saviles of importance that are in existence at
the present time in the male, line in the
parish of Halifax, or even in the West
Riding. Sir John Savile of Methley, . in
1765, was created Earl of Mexborough, and
was ancestor of the present Earl Who still
possesses large property in Elland and the
neighbourhood.

Sir Henry Savile, brother of the judge, is
said to have been born at Bradley, on 30th
Nov., 1549. He, like his brother, went to
Brazenose College, Oxford, in 1561, and
became a Fellow of Merton College, 1565,
taking his M.A. degree in 1570. He was a
mathematician and a Greek scholar, and in
1585 was elected Warden of Merton, and
eleven years after Provost of Eton College.
Having lost his only son in 1604, he spent
his money in bringing out an edition of St.
Chrysostom

on which he is said to have expended £8000.
He died 19th February, 1622 and was buried
at Eton. Mr. Hunter sap: "taking him
altogether he is the most illustrious person
that the County of York has yet produced."

The youngest of the three brothers, Thomas
Savile, was educated at Merton College,
Oxford, and became fellow in 1580 and
proctor in 1592 He was also very learned but
died young, and was buried in Merton
College Chapel in 1593.

THE CLAYS OF CLAY HOUSE.

This family was settled at Clay House from
a very early period. Deeds are in ' existence
tracing it back there to 1313. At the Poll Tax
in 1379 Robert Clay is described as a
merchant. We have the will at York of John
Clay, of Clay House: ' yeoman, in 1556. His
eldest son, John

Clay, seems to have married, according to the" Elland register, Mariola (properly Margery) Savile, sister of Sir John and Sir Henry Savile. He probably was buried 19th June, 1616. He had an eldest son also John, and a younger son Dr. Robert Clay, Vicar of Halifax, who was educated at Merton College, Oxford, where he took his doctor's degree, 19th July, 1609. His relationship to the Saviles probably got him the Vicarage to which he was presented ' in March, 1623. Little is known of him, excepting that he had articles exhibited against him which are mentioned in Watson's History, but they never were proved. He had, however, a good account in the Halifax register when he died, 9th April, 1628. He was buried in the library which he is said to have built. His will is at York. He mentions his wife Jane, a

daughter of Mr. Richard Wenman, of Oxfordshire, also his deceased wife. He had two sons, whom he wanted to be brought up in learning and in the feat of God, also a daughter Elizabeth. His books were to be divided between his sons, but if neither of them proved scholars they were to be sold. He left to Merton College £100 for two sermons to be preached yearly by a Yorkshireman if fellow or chaplain in the College, mention to be made of him (the testator) in them. He ends his will. " As‘a father, I leave this last chardge to my’ sonnes; to avoid drunkenes, tobaccho and swearing, and profaning of the Saboth ."

The last of the Clays of Clay House was buried at Elland, 15th April, 1693. The estate was then no doubt sold ; it ultimately came into the possession of the Wheelwright Charity. For some time the Dyson family resided at the house, and various tenants have since inhabited it.

In its best days it must have been one of the most picturesque houses in the parish of Halifax, but now, alas, with its proximity to great mills it is quite spoilt as a residence.

THE RAMSDENS OF GREETLAND

were a very numerous family there and are often mentioned in the registers. There was the branch which went to Longley Hall from which Sir John William Ramsden descends, in addition to the branches at Bowers, Crawstone, High Trees, &c. Many of these have probably died out, but the Crawstone Ramsdens are yet in existence, though under a different name. There was a Gilbert Ramsden who lived at Crawstone and died 28th April, 1629. From him descended Joseph Ramsden, who was buried 30th Jan., 16845. He was twice married; by his first wife he had John of Crawstone, who married Bridget, daughter of Walter Calverley of Calverley. Oliver Heywood

says of him that he was very fat and had
£1,000 per annum. He had no children, and
his brother Thomas succeeded, who, also,
according to Heywood, died young, having
shortened his days by intemperance. By the
second marriage, if our surmises are correct,
Joseph Ramsden was the father of Grace
Ramsden, who left the well-known charity.
She was baptised at Elland, 6th October,
1682, and made her' will 13th December,
1734. A full "extract is in Watson. Returning
to Thomas, just mentioned, his son" Thomas
was High Sheriff of Yorkshire in 1725, and
married Frances, daughter of Sir ' Walter
Hawksworth of Hawksworth. His son
Walter assumed the name of Hawksworth,
and his son, Walter Ramsden Hawksworth,
on inheriting the Farnley property took the
name of Fawkes. From him descends the
present owner of that charming estate on the
banks of the Wharfe.

Geoffrey Ramsden of Greetland, belonged
to another branch. He died in 1612, having
sent three sons to the University. Hugh, the
eldest, was baptised at Elland, 17th March,
1593-4; became Fellow of Merton College
Oxford, and Rector of Methley. He then, in
1628, was made Vicar of Halifax,
succeeding Dr. Robert Clay. His preferment
did not! last very long as he 'died the year
after, being buried in Halifax Church, 19th
July, 1629. It is not often that two brothers
succeed one another, but Henry Ramsden
was appointed to the same office. He also
had been baptised at Elland, and was
educated at Magdalen College, Oxford, bein
g also a Fellow of Lincoln College. He
remained at Halifax nearly nine years, and
was also buried in the chancel in 1638. His
wife, Anah Foxcroft, survived him a long
time and was buried at Elland in 1682.

Oliver Heywood makes the remark in
recording her death : " a good woman."

THE HANSONS

were a family of attorneys who perhaps
properly belonged to Rastrick as they lived
at Woodhouse. One member, however,
Nicholas Hanson, lived in Elland and left a
very quaint will, from which some extracts
may be interesting. It was dated 16th
September, 1613. He calls himself one of
the servants and clerks of the late Right
Worshipful Sir John Savile, Knight. one of
the Barons of his Majesty's Court of
Exchequer. His body was to be buried in the
churchyard of Elland, near the place where
his late father, John Hanson, of Woodhouse,
was buried. He mentions that he had only
one son and one daughter, both of which he
had carefully educated and preferred, his son
being one of the fellows of Magdalen
College in Oxford, and his daughter

married to his great comfort, " and whereas
it hath pleased God since my said sonne was
chosen fellowe of Magdalen College that
either by too much study and paines taken
att his bookes or by the abundance of
melancholly regninge in his body or by
whatsoever accident (to me unknowne) he
hath fallen into such a distempaure and
kynde of inlirmite by fitts, that he is neither
able to governe himself nor his place, the
case whereof hath been very chargeable unto
me 'and that he is att this present much
reformed and amended, and my hope is that
God will of His inhnite goodness in short
tyme restore him to his former health. My
humble request is to the Right Worshipfull
Mr. Doctor Langton, President of that
Colledge, and to all the fellowes of the same
house that they would be pleased seeinge the
lyke accident hathe

happened to many better men than my sonne
is and may hereafter happen to

others, to make one more tryall of my said
sonne from the tyme of absence already
given him in cureing of his mallady and
recovreing of his health by his frendes
industrie if soe the Lord shall please, before
they displace him of his fellowship which I
trust they will Consider," He gives to the
churchwardens of Elland twenty shillings
yearly towards the maintenance of a.
preacher, and to the poor twenty shillings
He gives his son Roberta ring of gold, his
best silver Cup, his desk and half the books
in his study, and his blessing' beseeching
God of his infinite goodness to restore him
to his perfect remembrance and sense. He
gives to his daughter and her son John Farrer
his best silver salt, double gilt, but Mary his
wife is to have the use of these during her
life. He also gives to his daughter a nutt
bound with silver, a silver goblet, and six
silver spoons ; to his son-in-law, John
Farrer, the other

half of the books in his study other than his President books. "I give to the Chappell of St. Matthew of Rastrick, one book conteyninge sermons upon the Apocalips of Jesus Christ. Item I give to my brother John Hanson the new satten dublett was my late maisters, and att his death bestowed on, mee, hopeing he Will for his sake and myne weere forth the same. Item I doe further give him a written Bracton in parchment. ' I give unto my brother Thomas Hanson to use dureing his liefe, and after Arthure Hanson his sonne my godson, the first volume of the Acts and Monuments. Item I give to my sister Judeth Deane after my wiefe her death the second great volume of the Acts and Monuments, see that she performe with me that shee sent me word of by my brother John. I give to cozin Thomas

Hanson of ,Brighouse a booke called " The Christian's Warfare " over and besydes such small books for Songe and Schollership as he and his brethren did chuse and take out of my books which songe books cost me moneys and I pray God bless them all and make us all his obieyent and faithfull servants." He gives to John Mitchell, to be delivered him when he shall be placed at Oxford or elsewhere, to his preferment my best new cloak which cost with the carriage 42s.6d., to his cozen Edward Hanson four of his President books, to his brother William Deane his book of " Resolution of a Christian." He had given his brother John Farrer a book teaching to learn to live and die well, and will lay out some English books for him.

The will was proved 17th December, 1613. The testator appears to have died on November 7th, and the inscription on his gravestone used to be in existence. We have no further information as to what

became of his son Robert, and if he ever recovered from his " melancholly."

THE WILKINSONS OF ELLAND.

This family became rather celebrated in the clerical world. There was a Robert Wilkinson, yeoman, who was buried in I 568, at Elland Church. He had a Son William who married Jennett, one of the sisters of the illustrious Sir Henry Savile. Her will is at York dated 1635. She divides a parcel of £20, a legacy from her brother. She mentions a kirtle of silk which was also a mourning gown for him. She gave her daughters her groggam gown, hat, ruff bands, and velvet stomacher.

William and Jennett had an eldest son John Wilkinson, who became D.D. and Principal of Magdalen Hall, Oxford. Another son William was father of another William, a parson at Adwick, and of Dr.

Henry Wilkinson, who was a noted preacher at Oxford in 1638. He was afterwards Canon of Christ Church and Fellow of Magdalen College, but was ejected in 1662. He spent the latter part of his life at, Clapham, where he kept an open meeting. The Adwick parsen had a son, another Henry. He also was D.D.. arid was Principal of Magdalen ,Hall, but was likewise ejected in 1662. ' ,He preached privately afterwards at various places under difficulties, and lived till 1690.

THE THORNHILLS OF FIXBY.

The Thornhills, of whom there are many entries in the registers, and, as stated before; many monuments in the Church, were descended from a younger branch of the Thornhills of Thornhill whose heiress carried the latter estate into the Savile family.

The Fixby branch by marriage or:

otherwise seem to have amalgamated all the lands of the Tothills and Fekisbys into one large property. From the time of Henry V. their pedigree is very clear, but they claim to trace back to a much earlier period. They continued in the male line till 1844. It cannot be said that there is much to relate concerning them. They were Justices of the Peace, and twice attained the dignity of High Sheriff ; they married with the neighbouring gentry, and till their final removal from the district probably lived quietly at home. Many of their members were educated at Oxford, (University being their favourite College) and at Gray's and Lincoln's Inn. Although probably a royalist by his connections with the Armytages, Sunderlands and Wentworths, John Thornhill of that date appears to have escaped punishment from the other side, as we do not hear of his being fined or of having his estates confiscated, so that he cannot have taken a very active part in politics. The last Thomas Thornhill left three daughters, between whom the estates were divided.

THE HORTONS OF HOWROYDE.

Although not now living in the present parish the Hortons may be considered an Elland family, as Barkisland formerly belonged to Elland ecclesiastically.. They were all christened and buried in the Church and several of their monuments are on its walls. They appear to have settled at Barkisland the end of the 16th or the beginning of the 17th century, William Horton who was buried in 1640, had two sons. The elder son William probably built the charming house at Howroyde, and was on the royalist side. His granddaughter Anne ultimately succeeded to the estate which she left to the younger branch who settled there. The second son Joshua, J.P., was a nonconformist and puritan, and lived at Sowerby, being a great friend of Oliver Heywood. From him descends the present owner in direct male line.

THE GLEDHILLS OF BARKISLAND.

The Gledhills were a very old family at Barkisland, and there are many entries of them in the Elland registers. There is a curious account of Thomas Gledhill, who was buried October 3Ist, 1617, and whose body was dug up and examined, because it was thought he had committed suicide. This, however, was found to be incorrect. In later times they intermarried with the Hortons, who succeeded to the estates. ' John Gledhill, who was buried in 16 56, most likely built Barkisland Hall, now unfortunately turned into a farm house. It \ was his daughter Sarah who left money to found a school at Barkisland, about which in recent years there have been disputes.

THE BROOKSBANKS 0F ELLAND.

They were an important dissenting family at Elland. John Brooksbank, who died in 1702, was a great friend of Oliver Heywood, who called him "a man of extraordinary piety and usefulness." His son Joseph went to London, and became of Cateaton Street, a warehouseman, citizen and haberdasher. He died . 11th June, 1726, and. was interred in the dissenters' burying ground at Bunhill Fields. In his will, 4th October, 1712, he left lands in Elland to found a free .school, which is at the present time in a flourishing condition. His grandson, another Joseph Brooksbank, of Hackney, 'in 1756, left "also a charity for dissenters in Elland. .He lived besides at Healaugh Manor, near Tadcaster, where his descend-ants still flourish, though they appear to have given ' up nonconformity.

Printed in Great Britain
by Amazon